Hilton Head Guidebook

Current Titles in this Series

Hilton Head Guidebook

Rebecca Kaufmann Crowley

Coastal Villages Press
Beaufort, South Carolina

Hilton Head Guidebook

Published by Coastal Villages Press, a division of
Coastal Villages, Inc., 2614 Boundary Street,
Beaufort, SC 29902, 803-524-0075, FAX 803-521-2000.

Available at special discounts for bulk purchases
and sales promotions from the publisher
and your local bookseller.

ISBN 1-882943-04-X

First Edition
Printed in the United States of America

For

the greatest artist

in all of

New Hampshire,

Jane McCorkle Kaufmann

Acknowledgments

Grateful thanks to Colin Brooker, Angus Cotton, Sheldon Fox, Charles Fraser, Bill Marscher, Fran Heyward Marscher, Bill Miles, and Michael Taylor for sharing with us their wealth of knowledge about Hilton Head Island and the surrounding area.

Written/researched by	Rebecca Kaufmann Crowley
Designed/edited by	George Graham Trask
Cover and illustrations	Jackson Causey
Maps	George Graham Trask
Research assistant	Constance Bowen Trask
Layout assistant	Margaret Holly
Copyreader	Penelope Rhoads Chitty

Contents

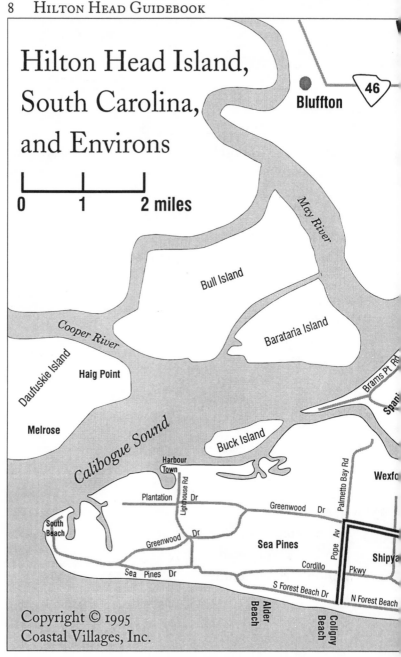

Hilton Head Island,
South Carolina,
and Environs

0   1   2 miles

Bluffton

46

May River

Bull Island

Cooper River

Barataria Island

Daufuskie Island

Haig Point

Brams Pt Rd

Spani

Melrose

Calibogue Sound

Buck Island

Harbour Town

Wexfo

Plantation   Dr

Lighthouse Rd

Greenwood   Dr

Palmetto Bay Rd

South Beach

Greenwood   Dr

Sea Pines

Pope Av

Shipya

Cordillo   Pkwy

Sea Pines Dr

S Forest Beach Dr

N Forest Beach

Alder Beach

Coligny Beach

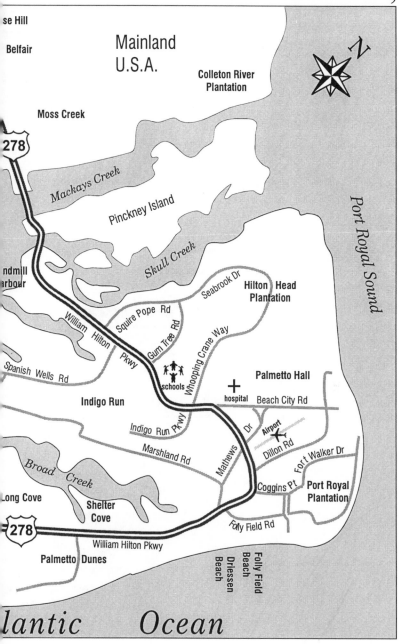

Welcome to Hilton Head Island

Welcome to Hilton Head Island, largest of the ocean-barrier sea islands along the South Carolina coast. The modern-day fulfillment of an extraordinary retirement and resort vision conceived only 40 years ago, Hilton Head boasts a venerable history reaching back to the earliest days of European exploration of the New World.

Over the centuries the island's population fluctuated radically. At the beginning of the Civil War tens of thousands of Union soldiers landed here in the largest amphibious invasion by U.S. forces until Normandy. Supplied by ships of the U.S. Navy, Federal troops and newly-freed slaves built a town on the island. After the Civil War almost everyone departed and the town disappeared. Reachable from the mainland solely by water until construction of a bridge in 1956, the island was inhabited in the first half of the current century by only a few hundred souls.

Do not be fooled by Hilton Head's contemporary veneer, which belies as rich and fascinating a history as any on the Atlantic coast. Discovered in 1521 by the early Spanish explorers—followed by the French, the English, and the Scottish—Hilton Head Island has seen many colorful dramas unfold over time. An intriguing cast of characters has crossed her stage, including noble Indian leaders, brave European explorers, swashbuckling sea pirates, daring Revolutionary War heroes, distressed plantation damsels, boisterous Civil War soldiers and sailors, crafty carpetbaggers, wealthy outdoorsmen, and visionary community builders.

This lovely island, now distinguished by first-class resort communities, luxury hotels, fine restaurants, and top-rated golf courses, was once the site of vast cotton plantations. In the first half of the nineteenth century cotton cultivation by slaves was the norm on Hilton Head Island. During and after the Civil War life here changed drastically. The slaves were freed, many leaving the island forever. Almost all of the old planter families were forced to sell their land and seek to rebuild their fortunes elsewhere. Eventually, the cotton plantations gave way to resort and retirement communities. Still, shades of Hilton Head's past live on, not only in tales told by her long-time black residents, but in her landscape, which speaks eloquently of unspoiled nature and an older, rural era.

Hilton Head's vast, sparkling beaches, sweeping marsh vistas, and gnarly, moss-draped live oaks seem almost primordial. As breathtaking a backdrop as these were for the simple abodes of her early settlers and antebellum cotton plantation workers, this natural landscape is every bit as compelling today, juxtaposed against her contemporary hotels and well-appointed retirement communities. Imagine enjoying all the elegance and convenience of a modern, world-class resort amidst the wild, awe-inspiring beauty of a maritime forest. Imagine golfing on one of the world's top 10 courses, while a lazy alligator suns itself near the ninth hole and large, prehistoric-looking sea birds circle overhead. Imagine playing tennis on a meticulously maintained, state-of-the-art court surrounded on all sides by age-old, towering oak trees. On Hilton Head Island there is no need to imagine, for these things are reality.

Here the best of God's creation and the latest of man's invention form a delicate balance. Old and new meld together to become something unique along the Atlantic coast of North America. Past and present. Tradition and progress. Nature and man. These are the essences of this singular place. Together, they make up the extraordinary paradox that is Hilton Head Island. Welcome.

Modern-Day Hilton Head

HILTON HEAD ISLAND is a foot-shaped barrier island facing the Atlantic Ocean on the southeastern coast of South Carolina, approximately 30 driving miles north of Savannah, Georgia, and 90 miles south of Charleston,

South Carolina. It is 12 miles long and five miles wide, encompassing 42 square miles of territory. Approximately 28,000 people reside permanently on the island, and 1.6 million people visit annually.

Unlike most other communities, Hilton Head does not have a focus that is immediately recognizable as the center of town. Legally, the island is a town, the residents having incorporated it as a municipality in 1983. But you will be hard pressed to discern a nucleus of public and private buildings such as town hall, court house, library, post office, parks, shops, and residences that are universally identified as a town center.

The reason for this peculiar circumstance has to do

with the course of the island's modern development and growth. Until 1956 the only way to get here was by boat. In that year a two-lane toll bridge was built. Later the toll was removed, and subsequently the bridge was replaced by the current four-lane one.

Before the bridge there were no paved roads, gasoline stations, shopping centers, golf courses, tennis courts, beachfront hotels, villas, conference centers, or any other accouterments of modern civilization. There was neither a telephone system nor an electric power transmission line. Following the Civil War occupation, the island was, for all intents and purposes, stuck in a time warp, covered in pine trees, inhabited by alligators, deer, and a few hardy black souls whose ancestors harked back to the days of slavery on the island's antebellum cotton plantations.

When Charles Fraser, the genius who invented modern-day Hilton Head, first envisioned an upscale retirement and golfing community here in the mid-1950s, he chose the extreme southern end of the island, creating Sea Pines on 5,200 acres. Because the only practical place to build a bridge was far away at the opposite end of the island, a two-lane paved road called U.S. Highway 278 (now four lanes wide with a landscaped median) was constructed from the bridge to Sea Pines. On both sides of the road were large tracts of undeveloped land, much of it facing the ocean, the sound, and the creeks. Highway 278 and Sea Pines became the driving forces in the pattern of development of these tracts.

Fraser envisioned Sea Pines as a place where people could live compatibly with nature. He wove streets around oak trees to save them; hired innovative architects to design houses that faded into the forested landscape; dug lagoons to create fresh water habitat and views on the inside of the island; and set oceanfront houses far back from the sea to protect sand dunes. Since he envisioned his community as being a part of nature and away from cities and towns, he did not realize that Hilton Head could grow to be a town.

Fraser soon discovered that golf, tennis, and condominiums could attract large numbers of people to his island paradise, people seeking vacations as well as retirement. He installed bike paths to get them from one place to another without having to depend totally on automobiles. Inside Sea Pines he built Harbour Town, with its red and white lighthouse, and South Beach at the extreme southern tip of the island, and proceeded to build more golf courses, tennis courts, and condominiums.

Fraser's success with Sea Pines prompted his father's former timber associates, Fred Hack and Olin McIntosh, to emulate the Sea Pines prototype. They controlled large tracts north of Sea Pines and founded Port Royal Plantation. Fraser and Hack soon found themselves locked in intense rivalry over development of other parts of the island. Soon, other developers arrived. All followed the successful Sea Pines pattern.

By the mid-1970s, a mere 20 years after the bridge was built, Hilton Head Island was covered with six gated communities, all borrowing features of Sea Pines and appealing to upscale retirees, vacationers, golfers, and tennis players. Then large hotel chains discovered the attraction of the island's oceanfront as a resort destination, resulting in the Hyatt, Hilton, Westin, and other hotels on the beachfront.

Each of the gated communities was conceived, like Sea Pines, as a world apart. But residents and visitors needed places to buy groceries and do everyday shopping. Standard neighborhood shopping centers and similar suburban sprawl grew up outside the gated communities. Then the "shop 'til you drop" mentality of the 1980s brought discount strip malls and an enclosed shopping mall to a population intent on making a visit to Hilton Head synonymous with a shopping trip.

Gated private communities, major resort hotels, and appealing shopping opportunities, all accessed from Highway 278, spread up the island and across the bridge to the mainland, where additional vast tracts of undeveloped land awaited. To link the southern end of the island more directly to the mainland, a long-sought "cross island parkway", first proposed by Charles Fraser in 1966, is currently being constructed. And a four-lane, limited access highway is being completed from Interstate 95 directly to the mainland approaches to the island.

The grand opening in mid-1995 of Sun City Hilton

Head, a huge Del Webb retirement community on the mainland 10 miles beyond the island, is the latest announcement. Plans for additional major development on the mainland are afoot.

All of which goes to explain why there is no center of town on Hilton Head Island. And why Hilton Head, which really is an island, has now leapfrogged, in name and frame of mind, to the mainland to include developments labeled "Hilton Head" that are miles away from the island. Accordingly, this guidebook speaks of Hilton Head as both the island and the nearby mainland.

The traditional black community on the island, whose history and heritage go further back in time than that of anyone else currently living here, continues to hold onto about 20 percent of the land, mainly in the smaller tracts farmed by their freedmen ancestors. They have seen their subsistence farming and fishing economy transformed by resorts and retirement communities, bringing schools, hospitals, better jobs, and all the challenges of modern-day America.

The success of contemporary Hilton Head Island is that it continues to hold onto its agrarian residents, continues to attract large numbers of visitors and retirees, and increasingly exports its lifestyle to the mainland beyond the island.

Hilton Head's History

THE NOW BUSY residential and resort island of Hilton Head has gone through numerous transformations over the five hundred years since Europeans first set foot here. Mankind's appreciation for this place goes much farther back,

 however, into the mists of pre-recorded history when the North American continent was home to indigenous agrarian people who migrated here millennia ago. For thousands of years before Europeans sailed to the New World, Indians lived peacefully on the shores of this large Carolina Sea Island, leaving behind few traces of their civilization besides Indian shell rings (the remnants of their circular dwelling areas). One of these shell rings can be seen today in the forest preserve of what is now known as Sea Pines.

The Discoverers

Following closely on the heels of Columbus' discovery of the New World in 1492, Spanish ships sailed up the Carolina coast in the early 1500s. The people living on Hilton Head Island then were almost certainly members of the Cusabo tribal group called Ewascus or Escamacu. Although earlier explorers may have spotted the high headland on Hilton Head's seaward side, the first Europeans officially to discover the island were the Spanish explorers Pedro De Quexos and Francisco Cordillo. In 1521 wealthy merchant Lucas Vasquez de Ayllon sent Cordillo on a trading expedition to America. While at sea Cordillo ran into fellow Spaniard De Quexos, a trader of goods and slaves. Slavery was not sanctioned by the Spanish crown, so De Quexos may not have confided to Cordillo his ulterior motive to capture Indians and carry them back to Europe as slaves. After landing on the coast and befriending the Indians, Cordillo quickly became cognizant of his partner's real intentions. A dinner party for friendly Indians on Cordillo's ship turned into a nightmare for all involved when De Quexos sailed off with the guests of honor.

De Quexos' underhanded abduction of friendly Escamacu tribesmen must have infuriated the gods because a strong hurricane arrived just as De Quexos was sailing away. As fate would have it, De Quexos survived the storm while Cordillo's ship was destroyed. The storm cleared on the feast day of Santa Elena (Saint Helen). As the sun came out, the suddenly pious Spanish captains named the entire area Santa Elena, claiming it for Spain and the Holy Catholic Church. The name survives today in a large body of water and a large island north of Hilton Head called St. Helena Sound and St. Helena Island.

This gesture of naming the area for Saint Helen did not placate Catholic church elders in Spain when they heard of De Quexos' slave trading, however. They reprimanded him for bringing Indians to Europe and ordered him to sail his captives back to America. The Spanish then made a futile attempt at colonization along the Carolina coast, but they ultimately left the area to concentrate on exploration southward.

In 1562 when Frenchman Jean Ribaut sailed here there was no visible evidence of Spanish presence. Ribaut claimed the area for France and set up a fort on a nearby island now known as Parris Island (home today of the U.S. Marine Corps Recruit Depot). To commemorate his claim, Ribaut erected a stone column carved with the coat of arms of the King of France. Ribaut's name for Hilton Head Island was "Ile de la Riviere Grande", referring to what we now call Broad Creek.

The Spanish, furious with Ribaut for intruding into what they still considered to be their sphere, rushed back to Santa Elena to rid the area of the grasping Frenchmen. By the time the indignant Spaniards arrived, all but one of the Frenchmen had left. Spain then decided to send some of its own citizens here to ensure that no foreign nation would take its land again (or so it thought).

Spanish missionaries lived among the native Indians, learning their language and teaching them Spanish. The Indians called Hilton Head "Escamacu", after the tribe that lived seasonally on the island. But by the beginning of the seventeenth century the Escamacu tribe had left permanently for the mainland, and the Spanish renamed the island "Isla de las Osas" or Island of the Bears. Though there have been no bear sightings on Hilton Head for a long time, we can assume that these furry creatures once splashed in island waters.

Arrival of Englishmen and Scotsmen

With the blessing of the Catholic Pope, the Spanish held this region without incident until the English arrived. In 1629 King Charles I of England named the entire region between Virginia and Florida after himself (Carolina) and granted this immense tract of eastern North America to Sir Robert Heath. Unfortunately for Heath, King Charles decided that the Spanish were not so bad after all and that the English did not need to colonize Carolina. Oliver Cromwell and other militant Protestants could not have disagreed more. These Roundheads were none too pleased with Charles' soft-hearted negotiations with a Catholic country, and disliked the idea of a monarchy in general. In typical seventeenth-century fashion, they decided that the best way they could serve their nation was to cut off the king's head and rule England themselves.

After much fighting and head-chopping, the royal line of Stuarts regained the English throne. King Charles II was a little more attuned to popular opinion than his father. He decided to expand the empire without regard to Spanish claims. He also knew that his head was more likely to remain attached to his body if he shared some of his royal wealth with important, well-armed nobles. In a "generous" gesture, he gave Carolina to eight gentlemen known as the Lords Proprietor, and encouraged them to settle the region. There was a stipulation that the Proprietors pay the king a small yearly sum for the land, along with one quarter of any gold and silver discovered. Since one quarter of nothing is still nothing, this arrangement did not increase the royal coffers as King Charles II had hoped.

In 1663 Sir John Colleton, one of the Lords Proprietor, sent Captain William Hilton from the island of Barbados in the Caribbean to explore the new Carolina region. Hilton was enthusiastic about the area and could not say enough good things about this vast island with a bluff headland where the game was plentiful and the soil rich. The island was later named Hilton Head in honor of this first Englishman to consider it worthy of serious colonization. Hilton's glowing descriptions did not convince British nobles to send colonists to the island, but his words may have influenced some of his countrymen. In 1670, a group of English settlers founded the town of Charleston to the northward, the first English settlement in Carolina. About 15 years later, Scottish colonists set up Stuart Town in the vicinity of the present-day town of Beaufort, which is located on Port Royal Island just north of Hilton Head Island.

Indian Wars and Pirates

In predictable fashion, the Spanish were extremely annoyed at what they considered the pilfering of land by English settlers. They sent Yemassee Indians up from Florida to terrorize the new colonists. The Yemassee were not a tribe to be ordered around, however. They decided to trade with the English settlers rather than massacre them. Some Yemassee settled on Hilton Head Island. Now the Spanish took matters into their own hands. War parties sailed up the coast, obliterating Stuart Town and causing great damage to Charleston.

Later, the dubious trading practices of certain English "Indian traders" disgusted the Yemassee to such a degree that they rebelled. Stories of trickery and thievery by traders included one that may have occurred on or near Hilton Head. The young men of a Yemassee village went off to fight on the side of English colonists against the bellicose Tuscarora tribe. While they were gone, English traders sold rum to the women and children of the village and took some of the Indians as slaves. When the Yemassee elders objected, the traders soundly beat them. Incidents like these infuriated leaders of the Yemassee tribe. Eventually the Yemassee were at war with their former trading partners, resulting in slaughter on both sides. After the Yemassee war, colonial leaders made some effort to maintain good relations with indigenous tribes, but eventually they forced most Indians westward.

Pirates were another threat to the safety of the English

colonists. The Sea Islands were favorite hideaways for ocean bandits. At first settlers tolerated, and in some instances even welcomed, the pirates. Merchants in Charleston were known for being especially hospitable to English pirates bearing large bags of Spanish gold. But by the end of the seventeenth century, these outlaws had stolen enough English property to convince most colonists that the rogues should be jailed or hanged.

The infamous Edward Teach, also known as Blackbeard, hid away on many of the area's Sea Islands and wreaked havoc in Charleston. He arrived in town one day with four hundred men, terrorized the townspeople, took prisoners, and demanded certain "medicines" in exchange for his hostages. Fortunately for his captives, these "medicines" worked wonders on Blackbeard's disposition. After taking a strong dosage of "medicine", Blackbeard let the prisoners go.

Throughout all these battles with Spaniards, pirates, and Yemassee Indians, the Lords Proprietor were remarkably unhelpful, sending little military aid to their colonists. In an act that foreshadowed the Revolutionary War, the South Carolina Commons House of Assembly declared the proprietary government overthrown and elected a governor of its own. This arrangement did not last long, but the British government did create a new colonial government that excluded the Lords Proprietor, placating the colonists for a while.

Permanent Settlement
and Revolutionary War

With all this turmoil keeping Hilton Head from being an attractive place to start a family, it was not until 1717 that the first Englishman permanently settled on the island. In that year John Barnwell started a five-hundred acre plantation in what is now called Hilton Head Plantation. Another resident of the area, Alexander Trench, grazed his cattle on the island. He liked the island and the melody of his own name so much that he called Hilton Head "Trench's Island", a name that caught on with early cartographers.

Many other families came to the island in the eighteenth century, including Baynards, Lawtons, Baldwins, Davants, Draytons, Mongins, Popes, Scotts, and Stoneys. Rice and indigo were their primary crops. The freshwater dikes of the Lawton family's rice fields are still visible in the Sea Pines Forest Preserve. Eliza Pinckney of Pinckney Island, an amateur botanist and plantation wife, was instrumental in the development of indigo as a Sea Island crop. The British government paid large subsidies to keep the farmers from selling indigo to the French. This may have brought plantation owners substantial sums of money, but they were more loyal to their disaffected fellow colonists than to their pocketbooks. Almost every Hilton Head planter supported the Patriot cause and many joined the battle against the British.

The planters on neighboring Daufuskie Island arrived from England later than those on Hilton Head. Unlike their neighbors, they retained their loyalty to the crown. The animosity between Patriots and Tories can be illustrated by an incident that occurred on Hilton Head during the Revolutionary War. A young bride, Mrs. Talbird, was tending to her baby one day when a group of Redcoats stormed up her front path to set fire to her house. She quickly handed the baby to its nurse and ran out to confront the British troops. Her anger changed to surprise when she saw that the leader of the brigade was her brother-in-law. Being a good soldier but a bad relative, he ignored her desperate pleas for mercy. He removed all furniture and valuables and burned the house to the ground. Slaves comforted Mrs. Talbird until her husband returned from battle. One can guess who did not get a Christmas present from the Talbirds that year.

Cotton Wealth

After the Revolutionary War, a new crop was introduced to the island that was to make the plantation owners wealthy beyond imagination. William Elliott planted the first cotton on Hilton Head in 1790. He put into practice his theory that if only the premium seed from the best cotton plants was planted from year to year, the crops would eventually yield superior cotton. A fertilizer of oyster shells, marsh grass, and silt helped the growth process. This long staple cotton—known as Sea

Island cotton—became world renowned and brought undreamed of riches to the island's plantation owners. At the peak of the cotton prosperity there were 26 plantations on the island. Cotton crops were more difficult to harvest than the indigo and rice previously grown, so more African labor had to be brought to the island. The Gullah culture of the island's black people, which combines aspects of African and European traditions, came into being during this antebellum period.

The new cotton prosperity allowed plantation owners to build grand houses in Beaufort, Bluffton, and Charleston, to which they retired during the oppressively hot summer months. During the remainder of the year the planter families on the island participated in such activities as hunting, fishing, and sailing. Celebrations with games and oyster roasts attracted visitors from neighboring islands. The Zion Chapel of Ease gave the plantation set a place to worship and marry, and a mailboat brought them news from the mainland.

Black islanders worshipped in praise houses on the plantations and lived in rows of slave houses called "streets". The living conditions of slaves varied greatly from plantation to plantation depending on the personalities and circumstances of the planters. Some planters educated their laborers, kept families together, and discouraged the use of force. Others, mostly absentee owners, allowed the overseers to split up families and housed their workers in small, dismal quarters.

Civil War Occupation

The old way of life on these plantations came to an abrupt halt with the start of the Civil War. President Lincoln believed that the key to victory for Union forces lay in the blockade of all Confederate ports. Port Royal Sound at the northern end of Hilton Head Island, halfway between Savannah and Charleston, was his first target. Naval Commander Samuel Francis DuPont and Army General Thomas West Sherman were sent down with the largest naval fleet ever assembled on this continent. Federal ships sailed in ellipses between the Confederate Fort Walker on Hilton Head Island and Fort Beauregard on Eddings Island. As the ships passed the Confederate forts, U.S. Navy gunners fired their massive weapons on the small rebel strongholds. Confederate guns were no match for the long range Union cannons, and the Confederate troops were vastly outnumbered. Six hours after the battle for Hilton head began, the rebel soldiers put up a white flag and boarded boats to take them to the mainland. DuPont and Sherman accomplished their occupation of Hilton Head Island in one day.

During the battle, Fort Walker on Hilton Head was commanded by Confederate General Thomas Fenwick Drayton. His brother, Commander Percival Drayton, captained the Union flagship *Pocahontas*. Percival Drayton was thus put in the unenviable position of firing upon his brother. It was rumored that the brothers spent the night in a Charleston church shortly before the start of the war, each unsuccessfully trying to convince the other to switch allegiance. After the Fort Walker battle, Percival Drayton went on to become a commander of the West Gulf Squadron in the Gulf of Mexico, where he was issued the famous order, "Damn the torpedoes, full speed ahead." His Confederate brother, Thomas, was given a desk job. Despite the hostility of wartime, Percival Drayton seems to have reconciled somewhat with his brother. Upon Percival's death, Thomas Drayton received the then substantial bequest of $27,000.

Once Fort Walker was evacuated by Confederate soldiers, Hilton Head became a massive Union base called "The Department of the South". Commander DuPont's ships brought 13,000 men, including a labor brigade of 1,000 former slaves who did much of the heavy labor necessary for the construction of military buildings on the island. All soldiers were put to work helping with the construction of buildings and fortifications. Fort Walker was rebuilt and renamed Fort Welles. Barracks, storehouses, a bakery, a hospital, a moat, and a customs house were constructed. Union officers occupied the plantation houses.

Planters and their families left the island before the battle, abandoning their homes and their slaves. Pillaging of the houses and the dead Confederate soldiers was done both by ex-slaves and by Federal troops. Commanding officers tried to stop their men from plundering, and they officially denied that their troops took part in this thievery. Eventually, the U.S. Treasury became the biggest plunderer of all by appropriating all the land and possessions of former plantation owners and selling them to help finance the war. Confederate raiders were infuriated by the mistreatment of their property and returned to Hilton Head at night to take food, items from their houses, and their former slaves. Some of the raiders also set fire to homes on the island and to bales of cotton ready for shipment. A former islander, Stephen Elliott, was credited with burning down 14 houses on Hilton Head in one night.

Entrepreneurs from the North soon realized that the island was a safe haven during the war, and that thousands of homesick young men would descend on Hilton Head with little to do except spend their military wages. Hotels and restaurants sprang up on the island, along with jewelry shops, bookstores, and photo parlors. A street aptly named "Robbers Row" was lined with these shops as well as more sordid vendors such as liquor stores, tattoo parlors, and tobacconists. Many a young sailor returned from his Hilton Head shore leave with an empty pocket and a pounding headache.

Another less savory aspect of life on Hilton Head during the Civil War was the smuggling done by less than honest Union entrepreneurs. Cargoes from the North included luxury items impossible for the Confederates in nearby Savannah to obtain by legal means. The smugglers loaded liquor, tobacco, opium, silk, and corsets onto marsh ponies which ran across the island to waiting barges. They made small fortunes on these midnight excursions, and as a result genteel Savannah residents did not suffer as much as most other Southerners from wartime blockades and rationing.

The period of occupation was an interesting one for black families on the island. The commanding officer at Hilton Head during much of the Civil War was a fervent abolitionist named General David Hunter. In May 1862 he issued a general order freeing all slaves in Georgia, Florida, and South Carolina, and he gathered together a regiment of black soldiers. President Lincoln quickly rescinded Hunter's proclamation, forcing him to disband the regiment.

The creation of schools for children of freed slaves was sanctioned by the U.S. government. Two such institutions were started in plantation houses on Hilton Head. A group of ministers and single women came down from Boston, New York, and Philadelphia in early 1862 to help educate black island children. The Port Royal Experiment, as this endeavor was called, gave the U.S. government a chance to see how the newly-freed families would respond to the transitions that the reconstruction era would bring to their lives.

The Civil War brought significant changes to the ownership of land on Hilton Head. Beginning in 1862 the U.S. Congress imposed a real estate tax on all occupied land in the area. Refusal to pay the tax resulted in the land being declared "abandoned" and sold to former slaves or Northerners. Since most Southern landowners were not about to risk their lives crossing enemy lines to pay the taxes, much of the land was sold, along with houses and furniture. At the end of the war most Hilton Head Island plantation owners returned to find their land sold and their homes occupied or destroyed. They were reimbursed $5 per acre for farmland that a few years earlier had brought them thousands of dollars a year in cotton revenue. In 1872 Congress passed an act allowing the former owners to repossess unsold land by paying wartime taxes, but by then most of them were too poor to regain their property.

Post-War Tragedies

After the war, Hilton Head Island suffered from the wave of poverty that afflicted all Southern states. The occupying Federal soldiers left for home. Abandoned plantation houses were stripped of furniture and boards by poor islanders. Plantation owners were forced to sell whatever heirlooms they might have in order to survive. Violent hurricanes destroyed many structures that had survived the war. Some people who had come down from the North for the supposed purpose of helping with reconstruction ended up helping themselves to anything they wanted. These opportunists were called "carpetbaggers" because of the satchels in which they carried their belongings, and presumably the belongings of others. Most of the old planter families finally left Hilton Head, and the descendants of slaves took over about 20 percent of the land on the island.

Agrarian Economics

By the end of the nineteenth century, many cotton plantations were up and running again, albeit on a much smaller scale, until tragedy struck once again. A small gray beetle called the boll weevil decided to make the southeastern United States its home. The insect's preferred diet of cotton bolls for breakfast, lunch, and dinner caused the destruction of cotton crops all over the South.

Many residents on the island turned to truck farming after the demise of King Cotton. South Carolina's growing season is later than that of Florida and earlier than that of the Mid-Atlantic states. Sea Island truck farmers took advantage of the time between the harvests in those two major vegetable producing regions to create cash crops that kept the agrarian economy alive on the island. Large-scale commercial oystering also became an economic mainstay with oyster factories on the island processing this produce of the sea.

Another industry that developed on Hilton Head in the early decades of the twentieth century was whiskey production. The 18th Amendment to the U.S. Constitution (outlawing the consumption of alcoholic beverages) only increased demand for Sea Island liquor. Distillers in these remote areas were not likely to be arrested even after the 18th Amendment was repealed. Many island families would not have survived the Great Depression during the 1930s without income from moonshine.

As island farmers tried to eke out an existence, wealthy sportsmen from up North bought large tracts of land on the island to be used as hunting grounds. Some of the best wild turkey hunting in the nation could be done on Hilton Head and surrounding islands. Wildlife flourished on the now quiet island, while the remains of large plantations and Union camps slowly vanished. The U.S. government retained about eight hundred acres of land at Coggins Point, where a fort was built but seldom used. Hilton Head Island became as sleepy and isolated as it had been for the hundreds of years before the Civil War.

The Great Awakening

In the early 1950s, two timbermen from Georgia, General Joseph Fraser and Fred Hack, discovered the potential of Hilton Head Island as a vast pine tree farm. They purchased thousands of forested acres on the island for timber. General Fraser's son, Charles, who was then a recent graduate of Yale Law School, accompanied the timber party on their visits to the island. While some in the party thought the island could best be used for timber production, others believed it would make an ideal hunting area for wealthy sportsmen. Charles Fraser had a better idea. He envisioned a community in which human beings could enjoy the natural beauty of the island as well as their favorite outdoor pastimes without destroying the natural environment.

In those days the word "environmentalist" had not entered the American lexicon, and the general practice of most developers was to tear down as much as they built. Charles Fraser recognized that Hilton Head's beaches, dunes, marshes, and forests were too beautiful to destroy and would actually draw residents and visitors to the island. But there was no bridge, and the island was infested with mosquitoes and alligators. By dint of inspiration and determination, Charles Fraser saved the trees, helped build the bridge, fumigated the mosquitoes, and subdued the alligators.

Charles Fraser, his wife, Mary, and his brother, Joe, built the island's first resort hotel, its first resort restaurant, its first golf course, its first tennis club, its first private school, and its first upscale shops. They enticed artists and naturalists to come here. They envisioned and created Sea Pines Plantation, Harbour Town, South Beach, the Heritage Golf Classic, the Sea Pines Conference Center, the Sea Pines Tennis Center. The houses blending into the trees, the boardwalks to protect the sand dunes, the bicycle paths to reduce the automobile traffic, the nature preserves to protect the animals—all were Charles Fraser's ideas.

Fraser's success with Sea Pines inspired others to mimic his concept northward on Hilton Head Island, resulting in a proliferation of other gated communities. And his example propelled others to create, with varying degrees of success, similar communities up and down the south Atlantic coast.

Since Fraser's initial effort, the retirement, resort, and tourist industries have taken over Hilton Head Island and the nearby mainland, making them one of the best known vacation areas on the East Coast. Over a million visitors come each year to enjoy the golf courses, tennis courts, ocean beaches, shopping, and wildlife of this magnificent area. But because of Charles Fraser, in spite of the people and the cars, nature has survived here.

Special Hilton Head Words

I
N OUR INCREASINGLY HOMOGENEOUS WORLD, it is
comforting to know that certain words give a sense
of place to special geographical areas. But deeply
understanding these special words inevitably re-
quires more than a superficial knowledge of the area. In
the case of Hilton Head, you cannot possibly be expected

to know its special
words unless you've
either lived here a long
time or had someone
explain them to you.
We've decided to save
you a lot of time and
confusion by defining
these words for you.

Calibogue. You must pronounce all four syllables of
this word. The first three syllables rhyme with the word
"calico". The last syllable starts with a hard "g" and
rhymes with "key". Until English settlers started agricultural plantations on the Sea Islands in the eighteenth
century, American Indians were the only people to live
on Hilton Head Island. They named the body of water
on the west side of the island (between the island and the
mainland) "Calibogue", probably derived from the Creek
Indian word for spring, "calaobe", all of which four
syllables are also pronounced. One of the antebellum

plantations on the island was also named Calibogue.

Daufuskie. Daufuskie is an Indian word meaning "land with a point," a reference to what is now called Bloody Point. This large island, accessible only by boat, lies southwest of Hilton Head Island and forms the southernmost of the barrier islands along the South Carolina coast. Until recently it was inhabited solely by a handful of hardy residents who prized most of all their independence from the mainland. In recent years portions of the island have been developed as low-key resorts.

Gullah. If you hear elderly black islanders conversing in a strange language that sounds almost like English, you may well be listening to Gullah speech. The term "Gullah" describes the language and the culture of the black people who have inhabited the Sea Islands since the eighteenth century. "Gullah" may have been derived from the name of the country "Angola", or from a tribal group in Liberia called the "Gola"; these are the areas in Africa from which the ancestors of many of the current black islanders originally came.

Gullah is a mixture of African languages, modern English, and old English. Missionaries who came from the North to teach slave children during the Civil War erroneously thought that the local language was merely English spoken with a heavy Southern accent. African customs practiced by black Sea Islanders include giving children African "basket" names, arranging homes in compounds with a central meeting area, hair tying or corn rowing, and basket weaving. Gullah culture has been the subject of numerous books and movies and is celebrated at events such as the annual Gullah Festival in nearby Beaufort.

Indian Shell Ring. Only 21 remaining Indian shell rings have been identified along the South Atlantic coast, three of which are located on Hilton Head Island. One of these, in the Sea Pines Forest Preserve, is accessible to the public. Indian shell rings are piles of oyster shells, arranged in a ring, that constitute the last tangible evidence of Indian villages along the seacoast. For thousands of years American Indians annually migrated to the coast from inland areas in fall and winter to live on the plentiful seafood. They built thatched huts in a circular pattern. Not burdened by the modern-day requirements of the Environment Protection Agency, they threw the remains of their oyster meals outside, the shells over the centuries of their seasonal habitation becoming heaped into a pile. The early English settlers especially prized these shell piles as a ready source of leached shell to build tabby walls and houses.

Live Oak. Although this may seem a foolish name for a tree, along the lines of "wet river" or "round circle", it is actually rather descriptive. The majestic live oak tree keeps its small, waxy green leaves year-round, unlike other members of the oak family that drop their leaves for winter. Gorgeous as these trees are alive, with limbs reaching out three times as far as their towering height, they are equally valuable as timber, especially coveted by boat builders for strength and resistance to rot. The U.S. Navy's early sailing fleet was built entirely from live oak, *Old Ironsides* being the most famous testimonial to the tree's strength. When Hurricane Hugo tore through the Lowcountry, it uprooted many huge, old live oak trees, evidence of the incredible power of that storm. Sad as this destruction was, it did have one positive result. Ship restorers collected fallen live oak timber from the storm and used it to restore such historic sailing vessels as *Mayflower II*.

Lowcountry. When you read visitor information sent by the South Carolina tourism board, you will see this area of the state referred to as the Lowcountry. The Lowcountry is the coastal part of the state and is low in relation to the hills and mountains of the rest of South Carolina. Due to its proximity to the sea and its low altitude, this region feels strongly the influence of the ocean and the tidal rivers and creeks. Millions of years ago, South Carolina looked vastly different, with the Lowcountry completely under water and with beaches along what is now the middle of the state. The ocean slowly receded, uncovering the lovely Lowcountry. Part of the Lowcountry is a series of islands—Hilton Head being the largest—located primarily in Beaufort County. These islands have been called the Sea Islands since Europeans first sailed along their shores. Sea Island residents in the Lowcountry feel privileged to live in one of the most beautiful regions in the United States.

Marsh. "You can't fool me," says the Northern tourist. "That's not a marsh, that's a swamp." Those Yankees, they can be so wrong. Marshes are tidal pastures teeming with wildlife, subject to refreshing diurnal saltwater tides. Swamps are stagnant places, freshwater sloughs gone stale. We don't have swamps here.

Once upon a time the entire Eastern seaboard was covered with marshes. Then, developers in the more industrialized states up North decided that these tidal pastures should be filled to make room for chemical factories and miracle miles. Now that Americans have finally come to realize that the existence of many species of fish and birds depends on these wetlands, most of the marshes near East Coast cities no longer exist. Luckily for the birds, sea creatures, and people who live on this island, Hilton Head developers had the vision not to destroy the marsh.

The marsh looks quite a bit like the African savanna, especially in the wintertime when it turns brown and gold. You won't see herds of wildebeest wading through the marsh grass, but there is enough interesting wildlife to keep naturalists entertained for a lifetime. Many forms of sealife begin their lives in the gentle waters of the marsh before heading for their adult ocean home. Many of our feathered friends build their nests in the marsh where they can feed themselves and protect their young.

People who live near the marsh are attuned to the changing tides and seasons, and feel a great love for these verdant wetlands. Spend 10 minutes sitting quietly on the bank of a marsh and you will never call it a swamp again.

Oyster Shells. For thousands of years, Sea Island oysters have been a favorite delicacy. According to local legend, a czar of Russia would eat only oysters that came from Daufuskie Island. The shells of these mollusks have not inspired quite the same enthusiasm as their contents, however, and have generally been discarded. In fact, the Indian shell ring in Sea Pines can be thought of as a large, ancient oyster garbage heap. These piles of oyster shells lay untouched until enterprising settlers came up with the idea to build houses with the shells.

They used the oyster shells to make a building material called tabby. Tabby is a type of ancient concrete made of burnt oyster shells (to create powdered lime), whole oyster shells, water, and sand. This material is remarkably strong, many of the original tabby structures of the early settlers surviving far better than wooden buildings. An example is the Stoney-Baynard plantation house on Hilton Head Island, which would still be standing today were it not for damage during the Civil War. Oyster shells were also used to make a fertilizer for Sea Island cotton. They were crushed, combined with decomposed marsh grass, and added to the soil.

Palmetto Tree. Because of its name, some folks get the impression that this is not a true palm tree. Actually it is a palm tree through and through, growing as high as 60 feet and living as long as 75 years, but without producing coconuts the way its relatives in the tropics do. The palmetto is the official state tree of South Carolina and is depicted on the state flag. South Carolinians are extremely proud of their palmettos. In spite of the fact that palmettos are actually palms, no self-respecting South Carolinian would ever call one a palm. It's a palmetto.

Plantation. Tourists may wonder why gated residential communities on Hilton Head Island are sometimes called plantations. During the eighteenth and early nineteenth centuries many large farms with distinctive characteristics throughout the United States, in both the North and the South, were called plantations. In those days the entirety of Hilton Head Island was covered in cotton plantations. Although only Shipyard and Spanish Wells have retained their antebellum names, all the present-day gated communities are built on the sites of old cotton plantations. It is only natural, therefore, that these large tracts of land are sometimes referred to as plantations. In deference to the sensibilities of black Americans whose ancestors toiled as slaves on these lands, many of the modern-day residential communities on Hilton Head have dropped all reference to plantation from their official names.

Sea Islands. Between the ocean and the mainland of this fair state are found hundreds of small islands called the South Carolina Sea Islands. While some of these (such as Hilton Head Island) face the ocean directly, most are removed from direct ocean frontage, surrounded instead by tidal rivers, creeks, and marshes. Covered with sand and forests, these quiet islands have served as hiding places for pirates and Indians, farms for English settlers, and now tourist destinations.

Until the mid-twentieth century, the only way to get to the Sea Islands was on a boat. This isolation from the outside world made Sea Islanders a different breed from mainlanders: more self-sufficient, more aware of tides and wildlife, and often more opinionated. It is no wonder that the Gullah culture flourished and still survives on these islands.

Sea Pines. This is the name of the first retirement and resort community on Hilton Head Island, inaugurated by Charles Fraser in 1956. Located at the southern end of the island, Sea Pines has become synonymous with Hilton Head Island. In the early years it was the only residential and resort destination on the island. The concepts pioneered by Fraser in Sea Pines were so successful that they have been emulated in the other resorts on Hilton Head and copied in communities all along the South Atlantic coast. Thus the name Sea Pines has spread to become almost a generic term for a particular type of coastal development.

Skull Creek. Although you may find this gruesome appellation completely inappropriate for such a lovely body of water, the Europeans who came to its shores obviously found something morbid about the place. Early maps of Hilton Head refer to this creek as "Golgotha", which meant "place of the skulls" in Hebrew. Later on, the name was changed to "Skulk" because Indians used to lie in hiding, or "skulk", along the banks of the creek before attacking British invaders. Still later, pirates sailed along the creek when they took refuge on deserted Hilton Head and it was called "Skull Creek" once again. More imaginative historians have postulated that pirates buried the skulls of their captives along Skull Creek, but there is no evidence that any such atrocities actually occurred.

Spanish Moss. That tangled, curly, light green net draping from our live oaks is more than just an ornament conjuring up memories of the romantic Old South. People used it as upholstery stuffing until they discovered its propensity to harbor "chiggers", which are little red bugs you can hardly see that itch like the devil. Birds delight in making their nests with Spanish moss. Contrary to popular belief, this plant is not Spanish, is not a moss, and does not hurt its "host" tree. It is an air plant that lacks interest in soil and dangles freely from limbs to catch sunlight and rainwater. If you decide to take some home with you, seal it tightly in a bag and heat it in an oven or microwave to kill the chiggers.

Spanish Wells. Although Hilton Head was named after William Hilton, an Englishman, the first Europeans to claim the island were actually Spaniards. They did not consider the island an appropriate place for a settlement, but they did recognize its usefulness as a source for fresh water. In the sixteenth and seventeenth centuries, Spanish vessels used the area around Broad Creek as a watering place on their trips up and down the East Coast. The name Spanish Wells stays with us today as a testament to the purity of the island's fresh water wells, whose acquifer even today provides the main source of drinking water for the island's residents.

The Heritage. After founding Sea Pines, Charles Fraser turned his attention to the sport that would put Hilton Head Island on the map. Fraser's research into the origins of golf in the United States confirmed his theory that Scottish settlers in nearby Charleston were the first golfers in the New World. He created the Heritage Golf Tournament, held each spring in Sea Pines, to celebrate the spirit of those sports-minded Highlanders. In so doing he brought Hilton Head to the attention of golfers across the United States and, indeed, around the world. Even though the tournament is now called the MCI Classic, it is owned and managed by the Heritage Foundation, organized in 1987. All profits from the tournament are distributed each year to local and statewide charities. To date, over $3 million have been given out.

"The Other" General Sherman. Anyone who has taken an American history course or seen *Gone With The Wind* knows about General William Tecumseh Sherman, the inflammatory Civil War pyromaniac who marched through Georgia to the sea, then turned north-ward to set South Carolina aflame. Few know that there was another Civil War general named Sherman, who commanded Union soldiers on Hilton Head Island dur-ing the early stages of the war. Unlike William Tecumseh Sherman, who gained notoriety as a man of action, our General Thomas West Sherman was a man of inaction.

T.W. Sherman was a veteran U.S. Army officer who served gallantly in the Mexican War. Unfortunately for the Union cause, this Sherman's earlier heroics were not to be duplicated on Hilton Head during the Civil War, for he seemed far more interested in engineering and food preparation than in leading his troops. Once Hilton Head was taken, he spent most of his time inspecting the buildings constructed by his men and tasting breads and pastries in the mess hall. T.W. Sherman's lack of initia-tive gave the Confederate Army time to regroup and build fortifications, and may have prolonged Civil War military operations in this area of the South.

Flora and Fauna of Hilton Head

W HEN THE TEAM of visionary planners and community developers first arrived by boat on Hilton Head Island in the early 1950s, they found a place inhabited mainly by alligators and mosquitoes. The island, the abode of thousands of Union soldiers throughout the Civil War, had reverted to a place of primeval beauty, seemingly untouched by man. Their challenge was to preserve this natural environment at the same time as they developed it. That so much of nature remains here is a testament to their success. Here are some of the more interesting creatures you may encounter:

Alligator. University of Florida fans aside, Southerners have historically had little fondness for this reptile. Alligators have been shot as pests, fried in batter, and made into boots for cowboys. Nowadays, alligators may not be well-loved, but at least they are admired and respected. These lagoon-dwelling creatures grow up to 15 feet in length, and weigh as much as five hundred pounds.

Winter visitors who look for alligators may be disappointed—hibernating season lasts until March.

Occasionally, a tourist from a large city, having seen alligators only in Disney films and zoos, thinks it might be "cute" to snap a picture of a friend sitting next to one of these creatures. Cute hardly describes the friend's expression when rushed to Hilton Head Hospital's emergency room with a severed leg muscle. Although there have been few alligator attacks on humans, these reptiles will bite you if provoked and have been known to snatch small dogs off their leashes for a tasty 'gator lunch. They can sprint suddenly and rapidly. So, bring your zoom lens if you want a close-up shot of this magnificent beast, and for heaven's sake leave errant golf balls in the water.

Blue Crab. This crustacean is a favorite snack for almost every creature on the South Carolina coast: gulls, herons, fish, and humans alike. Blue crabs can be found in the ocean, creeks, marshes, and fresh water ponds. Crabbing is a livelihood for some Lowcountry residents, so please do not disturb crab traps of others. These commercial crab traps are often tied to large plastic bottles floating in creeks. If you want to catch your own crabs, tie chicken parts to the end of a weighted string and drop it off the end of a dock. When you feel a tug, gently pull the string up. Throw back into the water any crabs less than five inches across the shell and females with orange egg masses on their abdomens. We need them in order to keep making more blue crabs.

Bottle Nose Dolphin. Dolphins are much like high school kids at the seashore. Natives of the area call these playful mammals porpoises. They travel in packs, play for hours in the surf, and communicate with each other in a language only they can understand. These sociable cetaceans can be spotted in tidal waterways as well as in the ocean. Many Hilton Head marinas offer dolphin-watching boat trips. If you see a dorsal fin coming your way while swimming at the beach and the theme song from *Jaws* starts playing in your head, look before you panic. It's probably a friendly dolphin. And anyway, shark attacks are so rare in these parts that you are more likely to shoot a 63 on the Harbour Town Golf Links than to be the victim of a "killer shark".

Brown Pelican. One of the most spectacular sights you will see on Hilton Head is the diving exhibition put on by brown pelicans. These birds fly up to 50 feet above the ocean and zoom down to the water with their bills leading the way. After a tremendous splash, the pelicans emerge with pouches full of water and fish. Salt water filters out through openings in their bills and they are left with a feast. It is difficult to dislike the pelican, which looks so clumsy on the ground and so graceful in the air. Many island residents have little stone statues of pelicans on their front lawns to celebrate their favorite bird.

Egret. The statuesque white birds that stand out against our marshes are called egrets. Three types are commonly seen here: snowy egrets, great egrets, and cattle egrets. As you may have guessed, the snowy egret is completely white, but then again so is the great egret. It will also come as no surprise that the great egret is larger than the snowy egret, but a large snowy egret can be bigger than a young great egret. The only way to know for sure which of these egrets you are looking at is to check its feet and bill. A snowy egret has yellow feet and a black bill, whereas the great egret has black feet and a yellow bill. Luckily for egret watchers and guide book writers, the cattle egret is easy to identify because it does not live in the marsh and has orange patches during the breeding season.

The Audubon Society, which is very active in this part of the country, had one of its first major battles over the egret. During the early part of this century, egret plumes in hats were all the rage. The newly formed organization of naturalists lobbied to make egret hunting illegal. Due to the efforts of Audubon members and changing fashions, egrets survived and still flourish in the Lowcountry.

Horseshoe Crab. Those brown helmet-like objects that your children don as they run up and down the beach are the shells of horseshoe crabs. Dinosaurs may be extinct, but these ancient creatures have survived for 600 million years, possibly due to their tough shells and tasteless insides. Neither a crab nor a horse, the horseshoe crab's closest relative is the spider, although in some functions it is unique. It can only eat when it is walking, with spines on its legs "chewing" the food. When exposed to air, the horseshoe crab's blood turns blue instead of red, as it contains copper instead of iron. This aristocratic blood is often used by scientists studying bacterial infections.

Jellyfish. Children who grow up near the ocean are constantly reminded to stay away from these squishy creatures. Jellyfish are very primitive animals (not fish) and can inflict painful stings that have been known to cause death in humans. The tentacles of jellyfish contain toxins which stun or kill their prey. The most common type of jellyfish in these waters is the translucent white Cannonball, which has a brown border and orange organs. It is not nearly so dangerous as the aptly named Portuguese Man-of-War, which is blue and has very long tentacles. People who are stung by jellyfish get red welts on their bodies and sometimes have allergic reactions to the poison. Sea turtles are immune to the toxins and love to eat jellyfish. Plastic bags lying on the beach look a lot like jellyfish to a hungry turtle, so please pick up any refuse that you see in the sand. Turtles do not survive the ingestion of a plastic.

Loggerhead Sea Turtle. From the late spring through the summer, the Sea Islands are honored with the presence of these magnificent, mysterious, endangered creatures. Late at night, female loggerheads crawl up on dark, quiet beaches to lay their eggs. The turtle digs a pit in the sand, lays as many as a hundred eggs, and covers the pit with sand. She does her work so well that unsuspecting beachcombers can easily walk over a turtle nest without knowing what they're doing. If you see what looks like the tracks of a small tractor in the sand, stay clear of the area. These "tire marks" are probably the trail left by the turtle's flippers. Turtle lovers patrol the beaches daily in search of nests, which can then be moved to a protected spot or covered with a wire mesh. If you find a nest, do not disturb it.

After a six to ten week incubation period, the eggs hatch and small turtles frantically make their way down to the sea. Predators both furry and feathered can quickly end a little turtle's life. Once in the sea, they can be caught in nets or eaten by sea predators. If a turtle does reach adulthood, it can live more than a hundred years and grow to five hundred pounds. No one knows for certain where these rare reptiles spend the majority of their lives, though we do know that they travel thousands of miles through the oceans of the world and that, somehow, the female turtle always returns to the beach where she was born to lay her own eggs.

Magnolia. Although it is almost impossible to find a rhyme for "magnolia" (control 'ya?), songwriters and poets who visit the South tend to fit the word into their lyrics anyway. And who can blame them? Magnolia trees grow up to 80 feet high, have large, dark green leathery leaves, and from summer into fall produce the most robust flowers you ever laid your eyes on. A true daughter of the Confederacy, the magnolia will forever be associated with the Old South. Just try pronouncing the word "magnolia" without a Southern drawl and you'll see what we mean, you all.

Marsh Grass. When you look out over the marsh, you may wonder how any plant could survive in such a salty environment. Marsh grass, a member of the spartina family, owes its existence in the marsh to its ability to excrete salt crystals. Decomposed marsh grass is an important part of the food chain, as it feeds the plankton that feeds the oysters that feed us. The next time you sit down to a seafood dinner, give thanks to the grass that grows in the marsh.

Moon Snail. Beachcombers often find beautiful shells with whorls of pink, peach, tan, and gray lying near gray strips of "rubber". These seemingly unconnected objects are the shell and egg case of the moon snail. The inhabitants of the lovely moon shells are aggressive little creatures that would make good subjects for a horror movie. Moon snails drill holes in the shells of fellow mollusks using a sharp, tongue-like apparatus that secretes an acid. After the hole has been made, the moon snail sucks the meat out of its living prey. The egg case, which looks like a priest's collar, is made of secretions of the female moon snail mixed with sand.

Sand Dollar. Pretty shells make good mementos of your trip to the ocean, but the ultimate prize for a shell seeker is an unbroken sand dollar. Like its relatives, sea urchins and star fish, the sand dollar exhibits five-part radial symmetry. Five little slots can be seen on the top of the sand dollar as well as five "petals" on the flower shape on both sides. According to myth, God created the sand dollar's holes to represent the nail and spear wounds of Jesus on the cross and the flower on the bottom to represent an Easter lily. If you shake a dead sand dollar, you will hear the rattle of "Archimedes' Lantern", which is really the dried-up central mouth. Live sand dollars are covered with a greenish fur which falls off when they wash up on the shore and die. If you find a live sand dollar on the beach, do future shell collectors a favor and put it back into the sea.

Sea Oats. Some of you who see signs cautioning against the collection of sea oats might wonder who would want to pick them anyway. We encourage you to keep thinking that way, unless you fancy a stint in the county jail. This valuable grass stabilizes the sand dunes, keeping them from blowing away with every strong wind. And without the sand dunes to protect them, the marshes would soon be filled with sand and made uninhabitable for marine life. And that would mean, you guessed it, the destruction of the natural habitat for many Lowcountry birds, animals, crustaceans, and fish. So don't pick a strand of those sea oats that look infinitely better on the beach than in your living room.

Shrimp. Although shrimp dishes now command top dollar in most Hilton Head restaurants, these creatures were considered little more than bugs until the twentieth century. Modern-day seafood lovers who think that the name "shrimp" does not do justice to their favorite crustacean can use the British word "prawn". Shrimp are goats of the sea, eating everything from algae and decaying matter to worms, crabs, and their own molted shells. You can easily spot the shrimp boats by the wide "arms" that pull the nets. Marine animals and birds often follow these boats in order to get an easy meal. In the past, dolphins and sea turtles were caught in shrimp nets, but now shrimpers must use retractable nets.

Points of Interest

ILTON HEAD'S MAJOR historical sites and nature areas are only a short drive away from any spot on the island. When visitors come to the island for golfing, tennis, or the beach, they often overlook these fascinating places,

which tell the story of the island before the resort and retirement communities of today were founded. To understand the island, you owe it to yourself to delve into this manmade and natural history.

Museum of Hilton Head Island, in the Hilton Head Island Chamber of Commerce's Welcome Center at 100 William Hilton Parkway, 689-6767, is the center of research into the island's history and ecology. Ongoing archaeological digs uncover clues to Hilton Head's past, while monitoring programs ensure the future of the island's wildlife. Visitors may take guided historical tours or beach walks led by the museum's knowledgeable guides. You can take a Shell Enclosure Walk to learn the ways of the island's earliest human inhabitants, the Indians. A walk among ruins of the Stoney-Baynard cotton plantation will give you some idea of what life was like during the antebellum period. Tours of Civil War forts demonstrate the importance of Hilton Head during this volatile period. The museum also offers nighttime loggerhead turtle excursions. Visitors can "adopt" their own turtle family for a $25 donation.

Historical Sites

Baynard Ruins are in what is now called Sea Pines. Two of the most prominent planting families on the island prior to the Civil War were the Stoneys and the Baynards. Both families settled on Hilton Head in the late eighteenth century and acquired almost seven thousand acres between them. These ruins were part of the plantation of Braddock's Point, which once stood where the western portion of Sea Pines is today.

Braddock's Point was a plantation originally belonging to the Stoneys. But somehow it was sold or transferred to the Baynards in the early nineteenth century. According to one Bluffton legend, a friendly card game between neighbors turned into a nightmare for John Stoney, who literally "bet the farm" and lost his plantation to William Baynard. The Baynards were not so liberal with their poker wagers and managed to keep Braddock's Point until the Civil War. After the war, a group of family members bought back much of the plantation from the U.S. government. However, these Baynards did not include all of their relatives in the repurchase of Braddock's Point. One member of the clan felt that she had been given short shrift, and sued the rest of the Baynards in order to regain her family's portion of the land. To satisfy her claim, the plantation had to be sold to an industrialist from the North.

The plantation home was made of a unique Lowcountry building material called tabby, which consists of oyster shells, sand, lime, and water. Tabby structures all over the Lowcountry have proved to be highly durable. The Stoney-Baynard plantation ruins are the last remnant of the antebellum plantation homes once on Hilton Head. Since these ruins are in Sea Pines, a $3.00 gate fee will be charged to all visitors.

Fish Haul Plantation Ruins, off Beach City Road. The first European to settle on Hilton Head, Colonel John Barnwell, started farming this land in 1717. Between the late eighteenth and early nineteenth centuries, the Drayton family purchased all of Fish Haul Plantation. During the Union occupation of the Civil War, Federal soldiers camped on this site. After the war the land was divided among the U.S. government, freed slaves, and members of the Drayton family. Eventually, the land was sold to Northern businessmen. The chimneys of slave dwellings are all that remain of a once bustling agricultural complex.

The most famous resident of Fish Haul Plantation was General Thomas Drayton. Prior to the Civil War, General Drayton exhibited his non-military skills by building the Charleston and Savannah Railroad and acting as its president. During the Union attack on Fort Walker, General Drayton commanded Confederate troops defending it while his Union brother, Percival, bombarded the fort. Before leading his men off the island to safety, General Drayton promised his slaves that he would return soon. When he did not come back, the slaves assumed he had been killed and composed a song about General Drayton riding to heaven on a white horse. Back on the mainland, General Drayton was alive and well and not allowed to go anywhere near a battlefield on a white horse. Although Fort Walker was lost through no fault of Drayton's, his superiors assigned him to a desk job for the remainder of the war.

Fort Mitchel, located in what is now called Hilton Head Plantation, was part of a mile-long earthwork fortification, designed by Major General Quincy A. Gillmore and built by Union troops in 1862. Gillmore is best known for his well-planned capture of Fort Pulaski near Savannah. He had the fortifications built as defense against Confederate attack from land.

The fort was named after Major General Ormsby M. Mitchel, who briefly commanded the Department of the South on Hilton Head in the early months of the Union occupation. He led the construction of housing for abandoned slaves from the Lowcountry who flocked to Hilton Head after the outbreak of the war. General Mitchel's career ended abruptly when he contracted malaria and died a mere four months after taking command. In addition to being remembered by the naming of this fort, General Mitchel's name was memorialized by Mitchelville, the first town in the South built by and for the newly freed slaves (see description below).

Fort Walker, located in what is now called Port Royal Plantation, was a Confederate fort taken by the impressive Union fleet in the invasion of Hilton Head in the early months of the Civil War. Union forces bombarded the fort by gunships. After the Union troops landed, they rebuilt the fort and renamed it Fort Welles in honor of Gideon Welles, the U.S. Secretary of the Navy. A moat was constructed around the fort, which became the center of a large military town. The fort city of Hilton Head contained all the amenities of home, including bakery, post office, blacksmith's shop, carpenter's shop, theater, church, printing office, and hotel. The infamous Robber's Row was located right behind the fort.

Nearby Fort Sherman was part of the remarkable earthwork fortification system described under Fort Mitchel (see above). It offered landside protection to Fort Walker. Access to these two forts is extremely limited for those who are not staying inside Port Royal Plantation, but a tour of Forts Walker and Sherman can be arranged through the Museum of Hilton Head Island.

Indian Shell Ring, located in the Sea Pines Forest Preserve. This ring, which measures 150 feet in diameter, is one of only a few such structures still in existence. As mysterious as it might first appear, the ring was actually used for the mundane purpose of trash disposal by the American Indians who seasonally inhabited Hilton Head Island until the European discovery of America. Most of the refuse has decomposed over the centuries, but the shells of oysters, clams, and mussels remain, as well as the bones of animals.

According to archaeologists, the ring was probably formed by the remains of food thrown by the Indians out of the thatched huts in which these people lived. The huts were built close to each other in a ringlike pattern for protection. Inside the ring was an area which may have been used as a gathering place. Just as later inhabitants were to do, the Indians who lived on Hilton Head left this area for cooler uplands in the summer. Spear heads, shards of pottery, and other Indian artifacts have been found near the site.

Mitchelville, off Beach City Road, was the first town in the South built by and for freed slaves. During the Civil War, thousands of abandoned slaves came to Hilton Head from Lowcountry plantations to gain the protection of the Union occupation. As there was not enough housing for these refugees, the Union commanders decided to construct barracks-like living quarters for the new island residents. About 1500 blacks lived in Mitchelville, where they were generally left alone to govern themselves. They built the village themselves, governed themselves, voted, had a police force, and conducted garbage pickup. The streets of the village were laid out in a grid pattern. The first compulsory school in South Carolina was founded here to educate the children. After the Civil War the residents drifted back to the farms they had fled or moved to cities. Today the village is gone, only an historical marker remaining to commemorate its existence.

Zion Chapel of Ease Cemetery and **Baynard Mausoleum**, Highway 278 at Mathews Drive. Prior to the construction of the Zion Chapel of Ease, planters on Hilton Head had to attend services at St. Luke's Episcopal Church on the mainland. In 1788, this chapel was built using funds from planting families, notably the Stoney family. Pastors from St. Luke's came to the chapel twice a month to deliver services to plantation families. The chapel was destroyed in the nineteenth century, stripped of its last boards by impoverished islanders soon after the Civil War. Soldiers stationed on the island during World War II supposedly ransacked tombs in the mausoleum searching for jewelry. The mausoleum and the chapel's cemetery have survived and can be visited today.

There is an interesting Civil War story connected with the chapel. In the aftermath of the fall of Fort Walker, much pillaging was done by slaves and Union soldiers alike. One plunderer must have stumbled upon the Zion Chapel of Ease, for the English silver chalices which had graced the altar since 1834 disappeared without a trace. Many years later, a tarnished set of "goblets" was purchased in a pawn shop far away from Hilton Head. When the new owner realized that he had acquired antique religious pieces, he promptly sent the chalices back to their rightful home on Hilton Head. Unfortunately, there was no chapel to which they could be returned, but they have been preserved at St. Luke's Episcopal Church in case the Chapel of Ease is rebuilt at some future date.

Nature Areas

Our unspoiled marshlands and forests are home to natural creatures of all shapes and sizes. Spend an afternoon away from the crowds in one of Hilton Head's wildlife or nature preserves and you will know what serenity really is.

Newhall Audubon Preserve, Palmetto Bay Road, 842-9056. Great naturalists such as Catesby and Audubon have been drawn to the wildlife of the Lowcountry for centuries. The Newhall Audubon Preserve lets visitors discover the beauty of native flora for themselves without the bother of wading through creeks and marshes. Meander down trails bordered by plants with such sultry sounding names as azalea, jessamine, Southern magnolia, and Cherokee rose.

Pinckney Island National Wildlife Preserve, Highway 278 at the bridge entrance to Hilton Head Island, is described in the Side Trips section of this book. This large area is home to most types of Lowcountry animals, reptiles, and birds, including many endangered species.

Sea Pines Forest Preserve, in Sea Pines. This six hundred acre preserve of pine, live oak, and other indigenous flora is a testament to Charles Fraser's love of nature. Seven miles of boardwalks and trails take the visitor past ponds of fish and waterfowl, alongside two-hundred-year-old grapevines, and by the ancient Indian Shell Ring. The wildflowers along Mary's Lane are a colorful springtime spectacle.

Whooping Crane Conservancy, inside Hilton Head Plantation. After the Civil War, impoverished islanders and bored carpetbaggers nearly caused the extinction of many species of Lowcountry birds by excessive hunting. Luckily for visiting ornithologists, the fortunes of the region improved in the twentieth century. You won't find any whooping cranes here, but indigenous birds such as osprey, egrets, herons and ibis abound. Bring your binoculars for an afternoon of bird watching. Charles Fraser is also responsible for establishing this nature conservancy.

Cultural Events & Entertainment

W HEN YOU FEEL THE NEED to broaden your activities on Hilton Head beyond shopping, going to the beach, playing golf or tennis, or viewing nature and the historical sites, you will discover a wide variety of art shows, musical events, sporting competitions, and festivals going on throughout the year. You can visit art galleries, attend performances by local actors or musicians, or watch your favorite tennis, golf, and croquet stars battle it out on the courts. Scores of volunteer organizations keep residents busy doing good works. And nighttime entertainment is offered by a variety of clubs.

Organizations

Cultural Council of Hilton Head Island is an alliance among 17 cultural organizations to promote the arts. They have recently raised funds to build a $12-million visual and performing arts center to be known as the Self Family Arts Center, located next to the Hilton Head Island Chamber of Commerce on Chamber Drive in

Shelter Cove. Scheduled for opening in the spring of 1996, the center will house a 360-seat performing arts stage and theatre; a visual arts gallery; a 140-seat rehearsal and studio theatre; a meeting room; and an art studio. This coalition helps its members and various other island groups to put on performances and exhibitions. Call 686-3945 for information about upcoming events.

Hilton Head Art League promotes fine arts on Hilton Head. The organization presents shows by local artists and brings works by nationally known talent to the island. Call 671-9009 for information about shows.

Hilton Head Chapter of the Barbershoppers sings old time melodies at island events. They have expanded the traditional barbershop quartet to include all island voices which meet their stringent requirements. All performances are suitable for family audiences. Call the Cultural Council at 686-3945 for dates and times.

Hilton Head Orchestra and **Hilton Head Jazz Society** present musical programs at various island venues. The Self Family Arts Center will be the scene of presentations when that facility is completed. Call the Cultural Council at 686-3945 for information about performances.

Hilton Head Playhouse puts on plays, dance presentations, and musicals throughout the year at their theater on Dunnagan's Alley at Arrow Road. Local thespians founded this organization in 1968 and have been entertaining residents and visitors ever since. After the Self

Family Arts Center is completed in 1996, the playhouse will present two hundred performances a year at that new venue, keeping the Dunnagan's Alley location as a children's theatre. Call 785-4878 for performance schedules.

Schedule of Major Annual Events

March

Spring Fest celebrates spring with festivals of food and wine, a college tennis championship, and a musical at the Hilton Head Playhouse. Call 686-4944 for more information. Many people believe spring to be the loveliest time of the year in the Lowcountry, with the azaleas and camellias in full bloom and temperatures perfect for a round of golf or a walk on the beach. Spring begins early here with seasonal flowers bursting into bloom as early as February 15.

Family Circle Magazine Women's Tennis Tournament is a favorite annual event of thousands of residents and visitors to the island. Over the years it has featured all the female greats of the sport, including Steffi Graf, Martina Navratilova, Billie Jean King, and Chris Everett. This tournament was a pioneer in women's sporting events, being the first all-women's tournament to be broadcast on national television. It is held at the Sea Pines Tennis Club the last week in March to the first week in April. Call 363-3500.

April

MCI Classic—The Heritage of Golf is South Carolina's premier annual sporting event. Over 1100 volunteers supervise the tournament, which is the first PGA tour event each spring following the Masters at Augusta National. Golf fanatics will want to follow their favorite golfer. Non-golfers can bask in the island sunshine and admire the verdant course and waterfront views. Spectators enjoy themselves to the fullest, with parties on the balconies of course-side houses and celebrations on sailboats around the 18th hole. Call 671-2448.

St. Luke's Episcopal Church Tour of Homes showcases a selection of Hilton Head's large modern homes built by some of the most talented architects in the country. This annual spring tour allows visitors to explore these contemporary masterpieces. Call 785-4099.

May

The **Croquet Southern Regionals** will appeal to spectators who wish to learn more about this unusual game. Croquet aficionados are not your typical sports fans. Beer and a hot dog may be all right for other people, but croqueters prefer a glass of chardonnay and smoked salmon. Don't expect to see cheerleaders or hear raucous chants from the crowds. The players, typically clad in elegant white, tend to behave themselves, making this a most admirable professional sport. Call 689-5600.

The **Bluffton Village Festival** is a yearly celebration during the month of May. Rows of booths run down the main street of Bluffton, featuring works of local artists and craftspeople. Festival goers can watch performances by local entertainers while they sample old fashioned Southern cooking. Call 757-3855.

Daufuskie Day is a reunion for friends and families of residents of that isolated island. Visitors can watch the sporting events, try some Daufuskie crab cakes, and bring a sweetgrass basket home as a souvenir. Remember, you can only get to Daufuskie by boat.

June through August

Tennis tournaments are held across the island during the summer months. The Van der Meer Tennis Center hosts its **Tennis Classic** in late June, while the Palmetto Dunes Resort hosts two tournaments: the **Del Monte Banana Open Doubles** and the **Junior Clay Championships**. Port Royal Racquet Club gets into the act in August with its **Rod Laver Mixed Doubles Tennis Tournament**.

Harbourfest at Shelter Cove Harbour starts in June and runs through Labor Day. Entertainment on week nights includes bands, fireworks, and shag dancing lessons. Call 842-7001 for schedules.

The **King Mackerel & Cobia Fishing Tournament** is held at Shelter Cove Marina in June. Fisherman from around the country compete to see who is king of the rod.

Day of the Child Tennis Benefit, a special tennis tournament, is held on the July 4th weekend. Proceeds go to help children suffering from muscular dystrophy.

September

Golf comes to the forefront of island activities again over the Labor Day weekend with the **Celebrity Golf Tournament** at area courses. You can watch your favorite golf performer drive into the same bunker that trapped your ball. Call 363-4653.

Festa Italiana celebrates the culture and food of that great boot-shaped nation. Listen to Italian opera, cheer the bowlers on at bocci matches, and fill up on traditional pasta and seafood dishes.

October and November

An Evening of the Arts auction is held in the late autumn, with proceeds going to island charities. This black-tie event gives islanders an opportunity to don their formal gowns and tuxedos. Call 686-3945.

The **Head of the Broad Regatta** may bring to mind the rowing competitions of Oxford and Cambridge, but Hilton Head is actually an ideal location for this sport of fine English universities. Rowers who have been splashed by icy British waters will be pleased to compete in this warm South Carolina river. Call 681-4207.

Nighttime Entertainment

Cheryl's Le Cabaret Piano Bar & Cafe, 13 Heritage Plaza, 842-7227, is a piano bar that showcases local musicians and dancers in a cabaret format. Sherman the chef prepares fish specialties and breakfast until midnight.

Club Indigo at the Hyatt Regency Hilton Head Resort, 1 Hyatt Circle in Palmetto Dunes, 785-1234. The only nightclub on the island, Club Indigo features live band entertainment and dining every night except Sundays.

Coconuts Comedy Club, 15 Heritage Road, 686-6887. If you didn't have enough laughs watching your partner's swing on the golf course, you may want to visit Coconuts. Stand-up comedians amuse Hilton Head audiences. After the laughter, you will sometimes be treated to live blues or jazz. A late night menu is available.

Quarterdeck, Harbour Town at the Lighthouse, 671-2222. Bring your dancing shoes for a night of beach music and rhythm & blues performed by the Simpson Brothers. Quieter souls may prefer to do their rocking in a chair on the patio while watching the sun set. Hungry dancers can try the raw bar, or seafood and vegetarian specialties.

Salty Dog Cafe, South Beach Marina, 671-2233. This casual Caribbean-style beach bar invites you to enjoy a drink under the sun or stars while you listen to songs by local crooners. If you get hungry, try their West Indian and Cajun dishes.

Wild Wing Cafe, Coligny Plaza, 785-9464. This favorite hangout among locals and tourists alike boasts 17 different wings recipes, claiming to feature the "best wings south of Buffalo". Live bands on the weekends add to the popularity of this beloved haunt.

Golf

THE SOUTH CAROLINA LOWCOUNTRY is the perfect setting for this game of the Scottish lowlands. In fact, the Scottish ancestors of South Carolinians were probably the first people to play golf in the New World, with clubs and

balls coming over on ships as early as 1746. The best known course in the area is the Harbour Town Golf Links where the vaunted Heritage golf tournament (now called the MCI Classic) is played yearly. The many other courses in the area are also favorites of golf magazines and tour professionals. All courses described below are par 72 unless otherwise stated, and lengths are in yards from the back tees. Many of these courses are located in private resort areas, so reservations are imperative if you want to get through the security gate. At golf-mad Hilton Head, it is always a good idea to make tee times as far in advance as possible.

Arthur Hills Course, in Palmetto Dunes off Leamington Lane, 785-1138. You don't have to choose between taking a walk along the beach or playing a round of golf here because you can do both on this course. Natural dunes and palmetto trees give this undulating course a decidedly beachy ambiance. Bring a few extra balls in case sea breezes send your drives into one of the ubiquitous lagoons. Length 6651, rating 71.4.

Arthur Hills Course, in Palmetto Hall on Fort Howard Drive off Beach City Road, 689-4100. Your short game will be put to the test on the new Arthur Hills course, chosen as one of the best newcomers in the country by *Golf Digest*. Those who are able to hit straight off the tee will be denied the pleasure of ball hunting among tall pines and moss-covered oaks lining the rolling fairways. Length 6918, rating 72.2.

Barony, Port Royal Plantation, Coggins Point Road, 689-5600. George Cobb created the Barony with small greens which test the accuracy of golfers of all skill levels. Wide fairways make this course playable for less experienced golfers, although they may have some trouble near the greens. Length 6520, rating 71.2.

Country Club of Hilton Head, Hilton Head Plantation, Country Club Court, 681-4653. A knowledge of high school trigonometry will be helpful in planning your shots around the elevation changes. If you need practice negotiating doglegs, you will get it on thirteen of this course's holes. Length 6543, rating 71.2.

George Fazio at Palmetto Dunes, in Palmetto Dunes off Carnoustie Road, 785-1138. Do not let a high score discourage you at this difficult course which is a favorite of low handicap golfers and *Golf Digest*. The long par 4s and 5s make you wish for John Daly's swing and the sand traps for Gary Player's chipping ability. Par 70, rating 74.2, length 6873.

Harbour Town Golf Links, in Sea Pines on Lighthouse Road, 842-8484. Don't pass up a chance to play the MCI Classic/Heritage course. Although more expensive than other island courses, the thrill of golfing on one of the world's top courses will more than make up for the dent in your wallet. As you walk up the oceanside 18th, watching the sailboats in the background, you'll almost be able to hear the crowds cheering at this most famous finishing hole on the entire PGA tour. Par 71, rating 74.0, length 6912.

Hilton Head National, Highway 278 on the mainland about two miles beyond the bridge, 842-5900. It is well worth the drive to play Hilton Head National, which has made the "top 50" lists of numerous golfing publications. Gary Player created this course with multiple tee placements and minimal hazards so that a wide variety of golfers could enjoy themselves. Length 6643, rating 72.0.

Indigo Run Golf Course, Indigo Run, off Indigo Run Drive, 689-2200. Golfers will feel as if they're on a nature walk on this Jack Nicklaus-designed course which blends in beautifully with the Lowcountry landscape. Length 7014, rating 73.7.

Island West Golf Club, Highway 278 on the mainland about seven miles beyond the bridge, 689-6660. Gregarious Fuzzy Zoeller actually seems to enjoy the game of golf, even while playing under the immense pressure of a professional tour. His golf course, which features rolling fairways and multiple tee placements, gives all levels of golfers a chance to shine. Instructional programs are available for adults and children from seven years up. Length 6800, rating 72.1.0

Ocean Golf Course, in Sea Pines on Tupelo Road off Greenwood Drive, 842-8484. Hilton Head's reputation as a golfer's paradise started with this beachfront course, originally created by master designer George Cobb and recently rebuilt under the direction of Mark McCumber to the tune of $1.5 million. Destined to be recognized as spectacular.

Old South Golf Links, Highway 278 across from Moss Creek on the mainland about one mile beyond the bridge, 785-5353. Three island greens and marsh views are the highlights of this nationally recognized course. As you play, stop to admire the views over the marshes and waters of Calibogue Sound. If you are not satisfied with your score, you can improve your game at the Ken Venturi Training Center. Length 6772, rating 72.4.

Oyster Reef, Hilton Head Plantation, Oyster Reef Drive off Whooping Crane Way, 681-7717. This long course was created by Rees Jones for residents of Hilton

Head Plantation. Congratulate yourself if you are not forced to three-putt on the large, undulating greens. Length 7027, rating 72.0.

Planter's Row, Port Royal Plantation, off Union Cemetery Road, 686-8801. One of the only island courses located in a non-residential area, Planter's Row gives you the feeling of golfing in a nature preserve. Try not to hit any of the deer or the birds which may alight on the fairway, and leave your ball in the lagoon if you spot an alligator nearby. Length 6520, rating 72.1.

Robber's Row, Port Royal Plantation, off Coggins Point Road, 686-8801, located near the site of Confederate Fort Sherman, offers players a Civil War history lesson in the form of descriptive markers at each tee. Approach-shot skills will be tested around the small greens. Par 72, rating 71.5, length 6778.

Robert Cupp Course, in Palmetto Hall, 689-4100. In an interesting twist on computer golf games that let you "play" real courses, award-winning designer Robert Cupp plotted this course on a computer. For a futuristic golfing experience straight out of *The Jetson's*, come play this geometric course. Length 7000, rating 74.8.

Robert Trent Jones Course, in Palmetto Dunes at Trent Jones Lane off Queens Folly Road, 785-1138. Water will never be far from your thoughts on this course, whether you are fishing your ball out of one of the 11 lagoons, or enjoying the ocean view from the 10th. For a real challenge, play this course when ocean breezes are up. Length 6707, rating 72.2.

Sea Marsh Golf Course, in Sea Pines on Willow Oak Road off Greenwood Drive, 842-8484, lives up to its name, with "marsh hazards" or marsh views on almost every hole. The slope of the greens and the trees lining the fairways test the accuracy of your putts and drives. Length 6372, rating 70.0

Shipyard Golf Club, Shipyard Plantation, off Kingston Road, 686-8802, a favorite of the Senior PGA Tour in the 1980s, features three "nines" that can be played in any combination. Lagoons come into play on many of the 27 holes. Length 6830, rating 73.0 (for 18).

Tennis

ILTON HEAD'S MILD CLIMATE makes it a perfect setting for year-round tennis, and accordingly some of the most prestigious tennis resorts in the United States are located here. *Tennis* magazine consistently ranks the is-

land's tennis centers among the best in the country. Whether you are new to the sport or a seasoned professional, an 80-year-old or a preschooler, Hilton Head's clubs have a tennis program to meet your needs.

Palmetto Dunes Tennis Center, in Palmetto Dunes at 6 Trent Jones Lane, 785-1151. If you are itching for a game but left your partner at home, let the Palmetto Dunes staff find a partner at your skill level with the Game Matching Service. Head pro John Kerr and his staff provide instruction with a variety of lessons and drills. Show off your newly improved game at one of the tournament competitions. Junior programs are available for the younger members of the family. 19 hard, 2 clay, and 4 grass championship courts.

Port Royal Racquet Club, Port Royal Plantation, 686-

8803. Start your kids playing tennis early with the "Hot Shots" program for 4 to 6 year olds. Programs are also offered for older children and adults. Bring the whole family to the Tuesday night festivities featuring exhibition matches, mini-clinics, fashion shows and more. Save a few dollars by taking advantage of the afternoon walk-on rates. 10 clay championship, 4 hard, and 2 grass courts.

Sea Pines Racquet Club, in Sea Pines at Harbour Town, 842-1893. Play on the same courts where the greats of women's tennis compete in the Family Circle Magazine Cup. USPTA Master Professional Kurt Kamperman directs the comprehensive tennis program, which caters to players of all ages and skill levels. You may get to rub tennis elbows with the great Stan Smith, who is the club's touring pro. This club was recently named the top tennis resort in the nation by *Tennis* magazine. 23 clay championship, 5 hard, 5 lighted courts.

Van der Meer Tennis Center, 19 De Allyon Road off Cordillo Parkway, 686-8804. Dennis Van der Meer has an international reputation as one of the best tennis instructors in the world. His offerings meet the tennis needs of the entire family with programs starting for children as early as age three. Nautilus machines are available at the nearby Player's Club for those who feel they need a little more power behind their serves. This complex also has swimming pools, Jacuzzis, and saunas, in which tired players can relax their muscles. 25 hard, 3 clay courts.

Van der Meer Shipyard Racquet Club, Shipyard Plantation, 116 Shipyard Drive, 686-8804, offers programs for players from 3 to 93. From the Munchkin program for tots to Senior Weeks for 50-plus players, all age groups are covered. A different stroke is covered every day in an hour-long lesson followed by a drill session. Round Robins give players the opportunity to compete against and socialize with other tennis buffs. 14 clay, 6 hard championship courts.

Other Fun Things to Do

T HE OLD SAYING "the world is so full of a number of things, I'm sure we should all be as happy as kings" may not have been composed by a Hilton Head Islander, but it certainly applies to the island. Visitors who want to extend their activities have plenty of attractions from which to choose. Boating, fishing, and water sports are natural pastimes for island dwellers. There are miles of biking trails on which to explore the island. And of course there's that wonderful beach.

Beaches

Nothing can beat a lazy day at the beach. Hilton Head has 12 miles of sand on which to flop. The beaches on the northern end of the island have coarser sand, while the ones on the south end have whiter, finer sand. The sand is moving from the north toward the south, despite the efforts of replenishment programs. Hilton Head beaches are hard packed, ideal for jogging or biking. Beachcombers can find myriad treasures along these sandy stretches, including crabs, starfish, horseshoe crabs, moon shells, and sand dollars.

Beach rules should be followed at all times. The rules for walking dogs and other domesticated animals are complicated, so be sure to ask before taking your pet for a beach romp. You may not bring alcoholic beverages, fireworks, vehicles, or horses to the beach. Wild creatures that frequent the beach must not be disturbed, especially the endangered loggerhead turtles and their nests.

The entire 12-mile stretch of beach is open to the public, but your ability to gain access over the adjoining private property is often restricted, depending on location. The following areas are directly accessible to the public and have metered parking. If you stay in one of the resorts, you will probably be able to use their beach access too. Don't forget your sunscreen.

Alder Lane, south end of the island off South Forest Beach Drive, has restroom facilities and vending machines, but the parking is limited.

Coligny Beach, south end of the island off Pope Avenue near Coligny Circle, is a favorite of the college set. Close to many of the larger hotels, it is a good beach for people watching and for showing off your new bathing suit. Plenty of parking.

Driessen's Beach Park (formerly called Bradley Beach), north end of the island off Highway 278 at

Bradley Beach Road, sports parking for 250 automobiles, as well as restroom facilities and vending machines.

Folly Field Beach, north end of the island off Highway 278 at Folly Field Road, is a popular beach with restroom facilities but limited parking.

Biking

Biking is the healthiest and to many the most enjoyable way to get around Hilton Head. This island caters to two wheelers, with public bike paths along North and South Forest Beach Drive, up Pope Avenue, and along William Hilton Parkway to Folly Field. Most gated communities, notably Sea Pines, have miles of bike paths for their guests. Rollerbladers and pedestrians are also allowed on the bike paths, so watch out for others. The hard-packed beaches of Hilton Head are perfect for biking at low tide if your bike rental company allows beach biking. So, strap on that helmet and give your legs (and lungs) a good workout.

Alligator Bike Rentals, 785-4346, rents bikes for adults and children, child seats, and tandems. Rentals are for three days or one week. Free pickup and delivery.

Bike Rack, 785-8777, rents beach cruisers and mountain bikes by the day and week. Free delivery and pick up.

Fish Creek Landing, 80 Queens Folly Road, 785-2021, rents bikes, tricycles, tandems, and in-line skates by the hour, day, or week. Delivery and pick-up.

Harbour Town Bicycle, Harbour Town, 785-3546. All your children's wheeling needs can be met here. Rentals of coasters, three wheelers, baby carts, high chairs, baby seats, cribs, rollaways, and strollers. Rollerblades are also available. Rentals are by the day or week.

Hilton Head Bicycle Company, 11-B Archer Road, 686-6888, offers cruisers, tandems, mountain bikes, children's bikes, and baby carriers. Free delivery and pick up.

Pedals, 71 Pope Avenue, 842-5522, rents bikes with many free extras such as child carriers, locks, and baskets.

South Beach Cycles, South Beach Marina Village in Sea Pines, 671-2543. Beach cruisers, tandems, and mountain bikes for rent with free delivery.

Cruises

Get the cobwebs out of your brain on a leisurely ocean cruise off the coast of Hilton Head. You can watch dolphins frolic in the surf and pelicans dive-bomb their prey. Visit one of the neighboring islands or the historic city of Savannah. Call all cruise companies in advance for reservations.

Adventure Cruises, Shelter Cove Marina, 785-4558. Sir Arthur Conan Doyle aficionados can step into the shoes of Sherlock Holmes for the evening on the Murder Mystery Theater Cruise. Professional actors and fellow passengers will aid you in finding the dastardly killer. Elementary, my dear Watson. Also offered are dolphin feeding, deep sea fishing, ecological, and Daufuskie Island cruises.

Calibogue Cruises, Broad Creek Marina, 684-7925. Prior to the construction of the bridge to Hilton Head, anyone who wanted to leave the island had to do so on a boat. Calibogue Cruises continues this seafaring tradition with narrated boat tours to Daufuskie and Savannah. This tour company is less expensive than most, but the boat rides take a little longer.

Commander Zodiac, South Beach Marina, 671-3344. Nothing alleviates the stress of an office job faster than taking a wildlife tour of the marshlands atop a gently floating Zodiac raft. Commander Zodiac caters to small groups of people, so you may take your family on a private dolphin watch and leave the crowds behind.

Outside Hilton Head, South Beach Marina and The Plaza at Shelter Cove, 686-6996, gives boat tours which highlight the beautiful scenery and wildlife of Hilton Head and surrounding areas. Take a sea kayak on a leisurely ride through marshes, down the Colleton River, or among the Sea Islands and watch the egrets and dolphins in their natural habitats. Outside Hilton Head also rents rollerblades and watersports equipment.

Vagabond Cruises, Harbour Town Yacht Basin, 842-4155 (*Vagabond*) or 842-7179 (*Spirit of Harbour Town*). Ride the Intracoastal Waterway to Daufuskie in air conditioned comfort aboard the *Vagabond*. The *Spirit of*

Harbour Town takes you all the way to River Street in nearby Savannah, Georgia, where you can spend three hours touring the historic district or just sitting at a sidewalk cafe listening to a blues band. Sunset and murder mystery cruises are also offered.

Fishing and Marinas

As seafood chefs in island restaurants can attest, the waters surrounding Hilton Head are teeming with fish. Deep saltwater fishing can be done at one of six man-made reefs in the ocean off Hilton Head. The closest to the shore is Fish America Reef at 32° 07.9' N, 80° 24.9' W, made of concrete pipe in nine feet of water. Hilton Head Reef is almost two thousand feet long in 50 feet of water at 31° 59.7' N, 80° 35.7' W. Other reefs include the deep Betsy Ross Reef (32° 03.2' N, 80° 25.0' W), the White Water Reef, and the Eagle's Nest Reef. Fish generally caught in these waters include mackerel, flounder, grouper, cobia, amberjack, barracuda, and sea bass.

Sailors from all over the world head to ports on Hilton Head. Island marinas are plentiful and offer docking for boats up to two hundred feet long. Boaters who wish to cruise the waters around Hilton Head will find peaceful rivers and creeks on which to sail. The Atlantic Intracoastal Waterway runs through Calibogue Sound to the Cooper, New, and Wright Rivers to Savannah. You can enter the waterway from the ocean up Port Royal Sound.

Marinas on Hilton Head offer docking facilities, sailing instruction, and fishing charters. Boaters and fisher-folk alike would be well advised to call the marinas in advance for times, availability, and prices.

Harbour Town Yacht Basin, in Sea Pines, 671-4534. The famous red and white lighthouse is a beacon to sailors. The circular marina at Harbour Town is surrounded by shops and restaurants. Fishing boats can be chartered for trips lasting four to eight hours. The Hilton Head Sailing Center gives instruction to sailors of all levels of expertise. Visiting boaters who can afford to dock here are considered resort guests and can use the Sea Pines facilities. 85 slips, boats to 130 feet.

Palmetto Bay Marina, 164 Palmetto Bay Road, 785-3910, is a large marina with floating wooden docks and two lifts. Seven inshore and offshore charter boats are available for rental. Boxed lunches and bait and tackle can be purchased at the marina store. Engine and hull repair. 125 slips.

Shelter Cove Marina, Palmetto Dunes Resort, 842-7001, a lovely marina on the Broad Creek, offers everything for the visiting boater or fisherman. Sailboats and powerboats can be rented and chartered. Sailing and water-skiing instruction is offered. The Ship's Store offers fishing and crabbing supplies and outdoor gear. 170 slips for boats up to 155 feet.

Skull Creek Marina, Hilton Head Plantation, Skull Creek Drive, 681-8436, is located across the river from

Pinckney Island on Skull Creek. Sailing charters offer night fishing, shark fishing, and dolphin watches. Visiting boaters can use Hilton Head Plantation golf and tennis facilities. Amenities include a travelift and service yard. 130 slips for boats up to 215 feet.

South Beach Marina, in Sea Pines on South Sea Pines Drive, 671-3060, has the look of a New England fishing town. The marina offers a large variety of charter fishing boats up to 60 feet, including charters for night fishing, bottom fishing, and offshore reef fishing. Stop by the South Beach General Store for all your boating and sundry needs. Sailing and water-skiing lessons are available. Boat and motor repair and painting services, 100 slips, maximum boat length 40 feet.

Windmill Harbour Marina, Windmill Harbour, Crosstree Drive, 681-9235. Visiting boaters who wish to dock in splendor should consider the well-protected locked harbor at Windmill Harbour Marina. Boaters who dock at Windmill Harbour are allowed to dine at the ever so private South Carolina Yacht Club. Some consider the club's cuisine to be the finest of any private establishment in the Southeast. 260 slips, boats to 70 feet.

Watersports

If you need a little more excitement in your life, why not go parasailing? You can also try your hand at other fast-paced watersports such as windsurfing, water-skiing, and jetskiing through one of Hilton Head's watersports centers. Visitors who like to take life a little slower can rent a canoe or paddleboat for a lazy afternoon.

Breakwater Adventures, Hudson's Landing, Squire Pope Road, 689-6800, rents cruisers and pontoon boats as well as waverunners and jetskis. Parasailing excursions can be arranged.

Fish Creek Landing, Palmetto Dunes Resort, 77 Queens Folly Road, 785-2021. Take an afternoon off and paddle through nine miles of rivers and lagoons at Palmetto Dunes. Fish Creek Landing rents out canoes and paddleboats as well as bikes and fishing equipment.

H2O Sports Center, in Sea Pines at Harbour Town, 671-4386. Learn how to water-ski, windsurf, or parasail from the friendly instructors at Harbour Town. Yamaha waverunners are available for rent.

Island Water Sports, South Beach Marina, 671-7007. No matter what your watersport rental needs, Island Water Sports has your equipment. Powerboats, sailboats, jetskis, and water-skis are all available for rent.

Island Scuba Dive and Travel, 130-B Mathews Drive, 689-3244. Why not become a certified diver on your visit to Hilton Head? Experienced divers can rent equipment from Island Scuba Dive and Travel and go on one of their diving excursions to a sunken ship off the coast.

Guide to Shopping

S HOPPING IS NOT JUST a rainy day activity on Hilton Head. Fashion plates from major cities drive hundreds of miles to save money at the upscale outlet malls. Some of the top names in women's and men's fashion have outlet stores on the

island and on the mainland near the bridge to the island. Visitors who prefer specialty shops and boutiques can choose from a variety of waterfront and village-like shopping areas. In short, shopping ranks among golf and tennis as one of the most popular sports for visitors to Hilton Head.

Specialty Shops

Coligny Plaza, south end of the island off Pope Avenue near Shipyard Plantation. One of the original shopping plazas on the island, Coligny Plaza features a large central area with pastel-striped gazebos and boardwalks reminiscent of a nineteenth century beachside resort. You almost expect to hear a barbershop quartet break into song. Lie down in a Pawley's Island rope hammock from **The Hammock Company** (686-3636) and you may never get up. This shop also sells other outdoor furniture, bird feeders, and nature books. On a windy day, buy a kite from the **Coligny Plaza Kite Co.** and head for the beach. Kids love **Magic Puppet and Toys Too** (785-3280), which sells toys by Playmobil, Brio, and Lego, as well as puppets, craft sets, and children's books. For dinner stop by **Alligator's** (842-4888), featuring fresh grilled fish and the best barbecued alligator ribs on the island. Pick up a box of sweets for your sugar at the **Island Fudge Shoppe** (842-4280). Art lovers should visit the **Red Piano Art Gallery** (785-2318) nearby at 220 Cordillo Parkway. Folk art from Southeastern states is featured.

Gallery of Shops, south end of the island on Greenwood Drive near Sea Pines Circle, is another popular shopping plaza. A popular island clothing store, **Porcupine** (785-2779), offers women's designer wear, sportswear, and shoes. Expectant mothers who need a pretty maternity dress or an outfit for their newborn child will want to peruse **Porcupine for Children** (785-6633). **The Ibis** (842-6646) is another spacious women's clothing store which sells casual clothing such as gauzy dresses that are perfect for hot summer days.

Harbour Town, in Sea Pines at the end of Lighthouse Road, sports the tall candy-striped lighthouse that has become a symbol of Hilton Head Island. Shops and restaurants encircle this famous boat-filled harbor. Harbour Town has playgrounds for children and outdoor cafes and benches for those who need a rest from shopping. Remember that Sea Pines is a gated resort; a $3.00 entrance fee must be paid to enter Sea Pines. Two **Camp Hilton Head** stores next to the lighthouse (671-3600) sell casual clothing including the largest selection of Hilton Head T-shirts on the island. Decked out in your new T-shirt, head over to **Harbour Town Chocolates** (671-6666) for a taste of their delicious confections, including famously sinful champagne truffles. Lick your fingers before entering **Harbour Town Antiques** (671-5999) where you can buy antique wildlife and flower prints by famous naturalists such as Catesby and Audubon. Pottery and porcelain shard boxes are also available. **Knickers** (671-2291) is a clothing store for gentlemen where the staff will attend to your every need. Sailors will want to stop by the **John Stobart Gallery** (679-2739) to view Mr. Stobart's impressive oil paintings of ships and harbors from Cape Town to Pittsburgh. Discriminating collectors of European porcelain and glass ornaments should peruse **Bailey's, Limited** (671-4715). Two especially-fine, locally-owned gift shops are **Nell's at Harbour Town** (671-2133) and **Harbour Town Crafts** (671-3643).

Main Street Village, north end of the island off Highway 278, is set up like the main street of a small New England village where people shopped in the days before five-story malls. Cheery geranium baskets line the walkways in front of the stores. The best known shop in the village is the **Cinnamon Bear** (661-5558), a country store filled with confections, teddy bears of all shapes and sizes, ceramics, and baseball cards. Nearby you will find the colorful **Creative Kitchen** (689-9460) which offers glassware and terra cotta in rainbow hues, as well as gourmet items for the kitchen. To buy the ingredients needed to test your new utensils, stop at the supermarket of Hilton Head gourmets, **Harris Teeter** (689-6255). If you want to dress up your home, **J. Banks Design Group** (681-5122) will attend to your interior decorating needs.

Mall at Shelter Cove, center of the island off Highway 278 across from Palmetto Dunes Resort, is an enclosed shopping mall. Inside you will find two upscale department stores: **J.C. Penney** and **Belk**. Women's and men's clothing can be purchased at perennial mall favorites such as **Talbot's, The Gap, The Limited, The Polo Store, Banana Republic,** and **Ann Taylor**. Specialty shops offering jewelry, soaps and fragrances, music, food, and furniture can also be found here.

Shelter Cove Marina, middle of the island at Shelter Cove Lane off Highway 278, has the atmosphere of a Mediterranean town with outdoor cafes near the docks and small clothing and gift boutiques. The wide, brick walkways are lined with benches and rocking chairs in which spouses of overzealous shoppers can relax and watch the boats. Fireworks are displayed here on summer evenings. R. Bolton Smith's **Harbour Art Gallery** (785-2787) showcases his bright, impressionistic landscapes of the Hilton Head area. The **S.M. Bradford** (785-3200) clothing store offers everything from casual cotton dresses to sequined outfits for evening. Dried flower arrangements and gift items can be found at the sweet-smelling **Bay Berry's** (686-2344). Outdoor ornaments such as wind chimes, stained glass pieces, and carved herons are sold at **Trilogy Galleries** (785-6747).

Sea Pines Center, in Sea Pines off Lighthouse Road, is another shopping area in Sea Pines set up as an outdoor mall. This center is on the way to or from Harbour Town. **The Island Bookseller** (671-3773) has a large selection of children's books, books on wildlife, Lowcountry guide-books, and the latest bestsellers. Across the way you can see watercolors and oil paintings created by local artists and find out about exhibitions from the friendly volun-teers at the **Hilton Head Art League Gallery** (671-9009). Dresses, bags and sweaters for those cool spring nights may be found at the **Acorn Shop** (671-4151) cloth-ing boutique. Collectors of fine jewelry shouldn't miss **Forsythe Jewelers** (671-7070), where you can find such rarities as a Picciole emerald ring, a three-carat yellow diamond, and antique mother of pearl pins.

South Beach Marina Village, in Sea Pines off Lands End Road, is worth a visit just for the view. Walk over gray weathered planks to the waterfront where you can see small boats in the harbor and egrets in the marsh. The outdoors **Salty Dog Cafe** (671-2233) sells T-shirts, san-dals, and Pawley's Island hammocks as well as cool drinks and island fare. Pick up sundries that you may have forgotten from home at the **South Beach General Store** (671-6784). If you haven't brought enough cool, casual dresses to wear around the island, stop by **Ibis** or **South Beach Boutique** (671-6200).

Village at Wexford, south end of the island off Highway 278 near Wexford Plantation. This pretty outdoor mall is filled with small specialty shops and informal eating establishments. Nature lovers visiting Hilton Head for the first time can find guides to the flora and fauna of the region at the **Audubon Nature Store**, (785-4311). Toys, games, and gifts for wildlife lovers are also available there. On the top level, **Smith Galleries** (842-2280) exhibit arts and crafts of local artists, including weavings, ceramics, blown glass, wooden kitchen utensils, paintings, and collages. Pick up a novel by your favorite writer and enjoy a light lunch at the same time at **Author's Bookstore**, (868-5020), combining a cafe and a bookstore. Your little girl will break hearts in a lace dress purchased at **Whitney's For Home and Kids** (686-2297). Handmade gifts and gourmet items are available at **Whitney's Gourmet Shop** next door. Sportswear for active men and women can be purchased at **Out Island Trader** (842-8988).

Outlet Shopping

Lowcountry Factory Outlet Village, Highway 278 across the bridge on the mainland, 837-4339. This large shopping area features many factory outlet stores for young, outdoorsy types. Clothing and footwear from **J. Crew, Bass, Eddie Bauer, Levis, Sam and Libby, Bugle Boy,** and **Reebok** will keep the sporting set well-dressed. Other stores offer men's, women's and children's clothing, sporting goods, silver, luggage, and more. **Brooks Brothers, Leslie Fay, Baby Guess,** and **London Fog** are among the other outlet stores in this complex.

Pineland Mill Shops, center of the island on Highway 278 at Mathews Drive, 681-8907. Fine clothing from **Adolfo, Ellen Ashley,** and **S & K Menswear**, fine china from **Royal Doulton,** and fine wine from **Pineland Liquors** can all be found at the Pineland Mill Shops. Four restaurants keep hungry shoppers on their feet.

Shoppes On The Parkway, middle of the island on Highway 278 near Palmetto Dunes Resort, 686-6233. If the terms "designer clothing" and "huge savings" sound mutually exclusive to you, check out Shoppes On The Parkway. Savvy city folk from up North stop on their way to Florida just to shop at these stores. If the names **Escada, Anne Klein, Carole Little, Ellen Tracy, Jones New York,** and **Harve Benard** mean anything to you, it would be a crime to miss the opportunity to buy your favorite clothing at cut rate prices. Other well-known shops are **Dansk, Van Heusen, Westport,** and **Player's World of Golf**. Next to Shoppes On The Parkway is **The Greenery** (837-3848), a bright outdoor garden shop filled with healthy plants and gorgeous flowers.

Places to Dine

WITH MORE THAN two hundred restaurants from which to choose, you'll never go hungry on Hilton Head Island. Chefs who have made this island their home have altered their recipes somewhat to make use  of tasty local ingredients. Many dishes start with seafood caught in surrounding waters and vegetables grown on nearby farms. The relaxed lifestyle on Hilton Head carries over to dress codes for diners, only the priciest places requiring jackets and making ties optional. However, patrons are expected to exhibit a modicum of decorum when they dine, so please leave your beach wear in your room. It's a good idea to call all restaurants in advance for hours of operation and reservations.

Formal Dining

Barony Grill, north end of the island in Port Royal Plantation at the Westin Resort, 681-4000 ext. 7555. The Barony Grill's hunt club atmosphere may seem out of place on this island of beach resorts, but hunting has been a favorite pastime in the Lowcountry since Indians populated the area. The aged Midwestern prime beef and Maine lobster on the Barony Grill's menu are favorites of discriminating diners. Dinner served every night of the week, reservations recommended.

The Gaslight, south end of the island at The Market Place off Sea Pines Circle, 785-5814. The best classic French cuisine on the island can be found at this garden-side establishment. Chef/owner Serge Prat, previously of La Cremaillere and the Rainbow Room, has spent almost 20 years on Hilton Head preparing fish, veal, and lamb dishes as only the French can do it. Reservations recommended, open for dinner Monday through Saturday, lunch Monday through Friday.

The Harbourmaster Restaurant, middle of the island at Shelter Cove Harbour, 785-3030. If you did not bring a jacket to Hilton Head, you may want to rent one for the evening just to sample the cuisine at this exquisite restaurant. Try the New Zealand rack of lamb, a tender veal dish, or an inspired seafood creation along with a bottle from the wine cellar. For penny-pinching gourmands, a three-course "Early Evening Preparation" is available if you arrive early. Open Monday through Saturday, reservations required.

La Maisonette, south end of the island in the Craig Building, Pope Avenue, 785-6000, serves classic French dinners, with specialties such as rack of lamb roasted in herbs and fresh flounder stuffed with crab meat. The fixed-price menu offers a variety of choices with prices lower than those of most other formal island restaurants. Reservations and jackets required, closed Sundays.

Dining Experiences

These restaurants can't really be considered "fine", although their menus rival those of any four-star restaurant on the island. You don't need to wear a jacket and you may just leave these establishments with some money in your pocket. Most of the following specialize in cuisine with a Southern flair, and all are highly recommended by locals.

Charlie's L'Etoile Verte, 1000 Plantation Center, 785-9277. Savannah native Charlie Golson has created a style of Lowcountry French cooking that makes full use of native ingredients. Choose among the myriad of fish entrees from the mirror menu, and enjoy your meal along with a bottle of French wine and freshly baked bread. This is our favorite restaurant on the island. Reservations should be made for dinner because it's a very popular place

Di Vino, Northridge Plaza, 681-7700, is the ideal place to propose to your sweetheart. This intimate restaurant serves light Northern Italian cuisine prepared by a former Madison Avenue chef. Toast your new life together with a selection from the extensive wine list. Reservations are a necessity if you don't want your plans ruined. Dinner served every night except Monday.

Julep's, The Gallery of Shops, 842-5857. The South has risen again. Julep's features contemporary Southern cuisine, with entrees such as peanut roast pork and bourbon grilled ribeye. Leave some room for a dish of key lime trifle or praline caramel custard. This is where the Hilton Head yuppies dine. Reservations recommended; open every night.

Rick's Place, South Island Square, 785-7425. If your taste buds start tingling at the mention of dishes such as herb and mustard crusted salmon with oysters and asparagus cream, you should sample the fare at Rick's Place. Award winning chef Rick Stone uses many traditional Southern ingredients, such as grits, buttermilk and local seafood, in his contemporary American cuisine. Reservations suggested; closed on Sundays.

Stripes, 114 Office Park Road, 686-4747. Those who think that "modern cuisine" means "tiny portions" have never eaten at Stripes. Dishes with an island flair, such as grouper in Jamaican jerk spices with mango chutney, are served in heaping mounds large enough for the most robust appetites. Reservations accepted; open seven nights a week.

211 Park Plaza, off Pope Avenue, 686-5212, is a new and trendy wine bar and bistro with highly-acclaimed food and wine. Enjoy quail, duck, fish, steaks, or shrimp smothered in grits while sipping one of their 72 wines available by the glass.

Seafood

Abe's Native Shrimp House, Highway 278, 785-3675. No one can prepare authentic Lowcountry cuisine better than an authentic South Carolina Sea Islander. The family that runs Abe's has lived on Hilton Head for generations, in which time they have perfected dishes such as smothered crabmeat and Lowcountry shrimp boil. Come here for a taste of the authentic South Carolina Lowcountry. Open for dinner seven nights a week.

Hudson's on the Docks, off Squire Pope Road, 681-2772. The seafood caught off the docks next to Hudson's is as fresh as you'll find anywhere on the island. This 25-year-old restaurant serves seafood broiled, fried, blackened, or stuffed. Entertainment is provided in the form of live bands and glorious sunsets overlooking the Intracoastal Waterway. Open daily from 11 A.M.

Crazy Crab, with two locations at Harbour Town and on Highway 278 at Jarvis Creek, 363-2722/681-5021. Visiting sailors will feel at home with this restaurant's old-style ship decor and will enjoy hearty portions of their favorite seafood dishes. Bring the entire family.

Mostly Seafood, Hilton Resort, Palmetto Dunes, 842-8500. If you love seafood but have had enough fried oysters and steamed shrimp to last a lifetime, come to Mostly Seafood. You can select your own fish and have it prepared to your specifications, or try one of the chef's fish or shellfish specialties. The chef is a "Certified

Executive Pastry Chef", which means you absolutely must save room for dessert. Reservations recommended; dinner served seven nights a week.

Old Oyster Factory, Marshland Road, 681-6040. If you love oysters, you've come to the right spot. This establishment was built on the site of an old oyster cannery overlooking Broad Creek and Shelter Cove. True shellfish lovers will salivate over the Factory Kettle, which contains lobster, clams, scallops, mussels, and shrimp. Open every night.

For Lunch

Cafe Europa, Lighthouse in Harbour Town, 671-3399. Have a French-style two-hour lunch with a good wine and an old friend in this lovely cafe overlooking the sound. The continental cuisine offered here includes salads, crepes, and seafood dishes. Also serves a late breakfast and dinner. Open every day.

Le Bistro Mediterranean, 302 Pineland Mall, 681-8425. You may never be able to afford a trip to the beaches of Southern France and Italy, but at least you can enjoy Mediterranean cuisine at Le Bistro. This intimate restaurant serves salads, pasta dishes, and light fare for lunch. Enhance your meal with a selection from their wine list. Open weekdays for lunch and every day except Sunday for dinner.

Market Street, Coligny Plaza, 686-4976, serves cuisine

of Greece, where the islands rival our own in beauty. Specialties such as gyros, mousaka, spanakopita, and Greek pizza will have you linking your arms and singing at the table. Open daily for lunch and dinner. Also serves breakfast every day except Sunday.

P.J.'s Incredible Edibles - A New York Deli, Shelter Cove, 842-5550. Homesick New Yorkers can stop by this deli for a hearty meat sandwich along with a fine European beer. Salads, desserts, and kosher food are also available.

Truffle's Cafe, Sea Pines Center, 671-6136. Stop in for a French bread sandwich and a bowl of the homemade soup on the way home from the beach or golf course. Seafood and pasta is also served, along with a selection of wines. Open daily.

Bakeries and Breakfasts

Carolina Cafe, Westin Resort, 681-4000, serves the most spectacular breakfast buffet on the island. Operating hours vary with the season so call ahead to confirm times. Also serves an elaborate seafood buffet at night.

Fish Tales Bar & Grill, South Forest Beach, 785-8253. What better way to start your day than with homemade pancakes or waffles on the beach? Omelets, muffins, home fries, sausage, and grits are also available. Open seven mornings a week from 7:30 A.M.

Hilton Head Bread Company, South Island Square,

785-4699. Hearty hearth style bread sandwiches and un-usual baked goods are the specialties at this new bak-ery/cafe. Muffins, croissants, and sticky buns are among the breakfast fare. Open Monday through Saturday from 8:00 A.M.

Main Street Junction, 1411 Main Street Village, 689-3999, is a popular local restaurant with an extensive menu, including eggs Benedict. Breakfast is served from 8:00 A.M.,also lunch and dinner.

Signe's Heaven Bound Bakery, 2 Bow Circle, 785-9118, offers Signe Gardo's highly praised baked goods. Maga-zines such as *Bon Appetit* and *Travel & Leisure* rave over the breads, cookies, and cakes prepared here. After breakfast pick up the fixings for a tasty picnic lunch at the beach. Open Monday through Friday from 8:00 A.M., Saturday from 9:00.

Skillets, Coligny Plaza, 785-3131, serves breakfast and brunch food exclusively from 7:00 A.M. to 3:00 P.M. Try a casserole of homefries, eggs, vegetables, and sausage along with Southern biscuits like mama used to make.

Places to Spend the Night

HILTON HEAD IS ONE of the most popular tourist destinations in the Southeast, and accordingly it offers a huge selection of overnight accommodations with almost 10,000 rooms, villas, and houses for rent on the island. High season begins in early spring and lasts until the late fall. If you don't mind wearing a sweater on the beach, you can save a lot of money by coming here in the winter. During the months of December and January it is not uncommon to see an enthusiastic Canadian tourist strolling down the beach in shorts and a sleeveless T-shirt; on many winter days the temperature rises into the seventies.

Visitors to Hilton Head tend to be outdoorsy types who have come here to enjoy their favorite sports and the beauty of the island. Developers realized the importance of sporting facilities and built many of their resorts and hotels with the active lifestyle in mind. Hilton Head's world-class resorts provide tennis courts, top golf courses, and a host of swimming and boating facilities for their guests. Even the small hotels offer golf and tennis packages.

Instead of staying at a hotel, many visitors opt to rent villas or homes. A "villa" on Hilton Head is a condominium or apartment, not an Italian-style mansion. Renters will often save money by renting a villa, but may not have the service or amenities available at a hotel. Renting villas is especially popular at the larger resorts, such as Sea Pines, where renters have access to all resort amenities. For assistance in choosing the type of accommodation to suit your taste, you may want to call the Hilton Head Island Chamber of Commerce, 785-3673.

Luxury Resort Hotels

Crown Plaza Resort Hilton Head Island, 130 Shipyard Drive in Shipyard Plantation, 842-2400. This world-class resort hotel offers 338 elegantly appointed rooms, including 25 suites, in its impressive five-story building. Each room and suite has a spectacular view. All are complete with coffee maker, hair dryer, and in-room safe. Individual reception stations offer guests a more private check-in and check-out. Amenities include ballroom, event space, restaurants, pools, and beach. Three nine-hole golf courses are a stroll away.

Hilton Resort, 23 Ocean Lane in Palmetto Dunes, 842-8000, features large, beautiful rooms with kitchenette. This resort is where serious golfers can test their mettle on the challenging George Fazio course. Less frustrating rounds can be played on the two other Palmetto Dunes courses, or you can skip the golf altogether and relax by a pool or work out at the health club. Watch the sun set from your private balcony after the game and spend your evening listening to a live band at the Regatta.

Hyatt Regency Hilton Head Resort, 1 Hyatt Circle in Palmetto Dunes, 785-1234. The wealthy plantation owners who once grew cotton on Hilton Head Island would be stunned by the opulence of this luxury hotel. Besides the fine golf courses and tennis courts available for use by guests, extras such as a valet service, a massage therapist, and sailboats make the Hyatt Regency truly a hotel for kings. The Regency Club rooms include concierge service, use of a private lounge, phones in the bathrooms, and complementary breakfasts, papers, and refreshments. Amenities include ocean-front dining at Hemingway's restaurant, serving fresh seafood, steaks, and chops, open nightly.

Westin Resort, Port Royal Plantation, 681-4000. Travelers who demand aesthetic excellence of their accommodations will want to stay at the exquisite Westin Resort. From painstakingly manicured grounds to perfectly polished decor, every inch of this oceanside resort is pleasing to the eye. Rooms have private balconies from which to view the ocean or gardens. Beach villas house two to three people and some include Jacuzzis. Guests can play on the tennis courts, croquet lawn, or one of three golf courses. Amenities such as restaurants, a lounge, a beauty parlor, and health clubs give the visitor no excuse to leave the resort.

Hotels

Best Western Ocean Walk Suites, 36 South Forest Beach Drive, 842-3100, has reasonably priced rooms with kitchenettes, mini-refrigerators, and cable television. The beach is only a short walk from the hotel, which is across the street from a beach access point. Guests may also take advantage of tennis courts and outdoor pools.

Radisson Suite Resort, 12 Park Lane in Central Park, 686-5700. A large recreation area will meet all your sporting needs. Besides the ubiquitous hotel pool, guests can use the volleyball, basketball, and tennis courts or the playground. Each suite has a kitchen, and many have fireplaces for those cool winter nights. Beachgoers can take a shuttle to the shore.

Player's Club Resort, 35 De Allyon Avenue, 785-8000, located right next to the Van der Meer Tennis Center, is perfectly situated for tennis fanatics. After matches, relax in the steamroom or whirlpools, or take a swim in one of the pools. Tennis and racquetball courts are on the premises. Tennis and golf packages are offered.

South Beach Marina Inn, in Sea Pines, 671-6498, is a New England-style village without the New England-style winters. These cozy rooms have such typically Yankee details as hardwood floors, throw rugs, and brass beds. Living room and dining room areas give visitors plenty of space to relax. Amenities include tennis courts, restaurants, shops, and beach.

Rentals of Villas and Homes

Coastal Home and Villa Rentals, 22 New Orleans Road, 785-6010, rents out villas and homes with one to five bedrooms for a minimum of three nights. You can choose from ocean or golf course views.

ESP Resort Rentals, in Sea Pines Center on Lighthouse Road, 671-4700, offers the very best homes and villas oriented to the ocean and to sports-minded vacationers in Sea Pines, Forest Beach, and Shipyard Plantation.

Palmetto Dunes Resort, off Highway 278, 785-1181, caters to fans of water sports with numerous swimming pools, boats for rent, and a private beach. Three excellent golf courses, a driving range, and tennis courts are available for landlubbers. Children will enjoy the playground and summer activities. Over five hundred villas and vacation homes of all sizes are available for rental.

Rental Management Services, 165 Triangle Square, 689-2501. This organization rents out villas in the Island Club next to Port Royal Plantation and at Villamere, next to Palmetto Dunes Resort. Accommodations have ocean and lagoon views, and access to facilities such as pools and tennis courts.

Sea Pines Resort, in Sea Pines, 785-3333 (Sea Pines), 671-1400 (Harbour Town), 671-6498 (South Beach). The first resort on Hilton Head is the ideal place for sporting families, active retirees, or people who just like to sit around on the beach. Golfers will want to rent a room for the MCI Classic and stay on to play the Harbour Town Golf Links afterwards. Tennis players can see the Family Circle Magazine Cup and work on their own games. The children's program keeps younger members of the family busy with outdoor activities such as swimming, fishing, and hiking. Hundreds of villas and houses are available for short-term rental.

Places to Live

AFTER A FEW DAYS of swimming and sunning on island beaches, hitting your three wood onto a perfectly manicured fairway, and indulging in the best darn seafood you've ever tasted, you may well wish that your time here would never end. Well, wishes can come true. Thousands of

people just like you—neither fabulously wealthy nor famous— have decided to live out their dream and make Hilton Head their home. If the idea of living and working here, retiring here, or having a second home here appeals to you, call the resort real estate offices (numbers given below), or phone one of the many real estate agents who work in the area. A free publication, *Homes & Land of Hilton Head Island*, will give you a good idea of property on the market.

Belfair, on the mainland between Moss Creek and Melrose, is a brand new addition to the list of prestigious places to live in the Bluffton area. Thirty-six holes of golf are planned on its one thousand acres, the first eighteen holes designed by Tom Fazio. Planned facilities include a golf learning center, a clubhouse overlooking the Colleton River, a swimming and family fitness center, tennis courts, a fishing lake, nature trails, and a wildlife conservancy.

Colleton River Plantation, on the mainland, 989-3131. Nestled along the Colleton River next to the South Carolina Nature Preserve, Colleton River Plantation contains just 395 exclusive single-family homesites on seven hundred acres. Exquisite structures are the norm here, one of the most outstanding being the Lowcountry-style clubhouse at the center of this golfing community's activities. Overlooking the final four holes of the private-membership Jack Nicklaus-designed golf course, this exclusive club sets a standard for others to emulate.

Haig Point, on Daufuskie Island, 686-4244. In times past, part of the romance of island living was the knowledge that your home could only be reached by boat. Those who live in Haig Point can appreciate this feeling. This picturesque community of Lowcountry homes is located on remote Daufuskie Island, which is only accessible by boat. Amenities on Haig Point include an equestrian center, a beach club, and a golf course which has won rave reviews from *Golf Digest*.

Hilton Head Plantation, north end of Hilton Head Island, 689-7100. Flanked by Skull Creek on the north

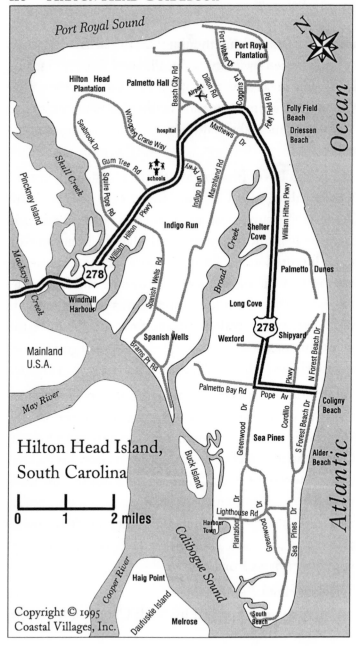

Hilton Head Island,
South Carolina

0   1   2 miles

Copyright © 1995
Coastal Villages, Inc.

and Port Royal Sound on the east, Hilton Head Plantation offers a wide variety of lots and accommodations on
almost four thousand acres of land. Those who live here
can enjoy viewing Lowcountry flora and fauna in nature
preserves, rotate golfing games between four courses, or
sun themselves for hours on two miles of beach. Boats
can be docked at Skull Creek Marina.

Indigo Run, north end of Hilton Head Island, 681-
3300. In this community you may wander alone through
forests of live oak and pine trees, admiring the views of
Broad Creek, without a visitor in sight. Indigo Run's
1,700 acres are completely private, meaning that no un-
invited guests are allowed in this community. Many
homes here have marsh or lagoon views, or look out over
one of two Nicklaus golf courses.

Long Cove, middle of Hilton Head Island, 842-2442.
Those who appreciate the finer things in life should
consider a home in exclusive, elegant, extremely private
Long Cove. Stately mansions and smaller luxury homes
overlook marshes, lagoons, and a golf course which is
consistently ranked among the top 10 in South Carolina.

Melrose, on Daufuskie Island, is the modern-day
equivalent of a club retreat for the wealthy. Available only
to its members, Melrose provides numerous facilities to
salve body and soul, including beach cottages, an oceanfront inn, dining, and a general store.

Moss Creek, on the mainland, 785-7177. Residents of

this 1,100-acre off-island community enjoy spending their leisure time in energetic pursuits such as golfing on a private Tom Fazio course, biking along trails lined with Lowcountry foliage, or sailing down the Intracoastal Waterway. The Southern-style homes in Moss Creek's neighborhoods overlook lagoons, marshes, and golf courses.

Palmetto Dunes, middle of Hilton Head Island, 842-1111. Just think of what your friends at home will say when you tell them that you have bought a home in a resort where notables from all over the world choose to vacation. In fact, you may find out that you have more friends than you ever imagined, once you introduce them to the championship golf courses, pristine beaches, and perfectly maintained tennis courts of Palmetto Dunes. An 11-mile lagoon system makes waterfront living possible for those who will never be able to afford an oceanfront home.

Palmetto Hall, north end of Hilton Head Island, 689-3333, is a 750-acre golfing paradise located near the island's hospital and public schools. Many residents are able to walk out the back door of their Lowcountry-style houses and onto an Arthur Hills or Robert Cupp course. Those who don't want to spend every leisure hour playing golf may go fishing in one of the community lakes, walk through the nature reserve, or sit out by the pool at the Palmetto Hall clubhouse.

Port Royal Plantation, north end of Hilton Head Island, is home of the Westin Resort and has some of the premier oceanfront property on the Southeast coast. If you have aristocratic aspirations, you may copy one of the exquisite mansions that have been built overlooking the Atlantic Ocean and Port Royal Sound, and be assured that your home is fit for royalty. Those with more limited budgets may live near the marsh or within "driving" distance of two George Cobb and one William Byrd golf courses. Besides golf courses, recreational amenities include croquet courts, three types of tennis courts, and a club on the ocean.

Rose Hill, on the mainland, 757-4945. The tranquil Colleton River flows by the two thousand acres of Rose Hill Plantation, providing a fertile fishing and crabbing ground for residents who want to be certain that their dinner has been freshly-caught. The antebellum Rose Hill mansion on the grounds sets the tone for newer homes built in Rose Hill. Recreational facilities include tennis courts, pools, a 27-hole golf course, and an equestrian center.

Sea Pines, south end of Hilton Head Island, 785-3334, the brainchild of Charles Fraser, was the first gated community to be developed on Hilton Head. This 5,200-acre community of magnificent homes surrounded by nature preserves, bustling marinas, quiet beaches, stables, shopping centers, bike paths, and world-renowned golf courses sets the standard for seaside luxury resorts everywhere. Residents who don't like crowds may want to go on vacation during the MCI Classic and Family Circle Magazine Cup weekends, but more sociable types will want to stay and join in the fun.

Shipyard, south end of Hilton Head Island, is a tennis and golfing community located on the ocean just north of Sea Pines. Homesites at Shipyard Plantation overlook the ocean, three nine-hole golf courses, and lagoons. Paths that run past the beach and by lagoons give joggers an incentive to add a few miles to their daily runs.

Spanish Wells, north end of Hilton Head Island, 681-2111. Although Spaniards of the sixteenth century did not deign to live on Hilton Head Island, they did draw water from the Broad Creek. Their American descendants can build a home in Spanish Wells, buy a sailboat, and explore the South Carolina coast themselves. Lots and homes in this private community afford lovely views of Broad Creek, Calibogue Sound, and Sea Island marshes.

Sun City Hilton Head, on the mainland, 837-2255. Del Webb Corporation's Sun City in Arizona has set the standard for retirement communities across the country. Sun City Hilton Head is Del Webb's latest venture, and should prove to be at least as successful as its southwestern sister. A lovely forested area of 5,600 acres on the outskirts of Bluffton will become a huge development of homes and villas for the over-55 age group. The homes in Sun City Hilton Head will be constructed over the next decade.

Wexford, middle of Hilton Head Island, 686-8800, is the Southern equivalent of aristocratic Newport, Rhode Island. Genteel families live in sequestered bliss on the five hundred acres of Wexford Plantation, where they divide their time between tending to gracious estate-type homes, meeting other residents for rounds of golf or gourmet meals at the club, and negotiating their sailboats through Wexford's canal system. And they say money can't buy happiness?

Windmill Harbour, north end of Hilton Head Island, 681-5600. Serious yachtsmen and yachtswomen should consider buying a home at Windmill Harbour. Boating is often on the minds of Windmill Harbour residents, who are able to take advantage of a state-of-the-art marina and the South Carolina Yacht Club, one of the finest yacht clubs in the country. If you just can't bear to leave your boat at the marina, you may buy a homesite with a slip and moor your precious yacht (up to 70 feet) right outside your back door. Those who can bear to stay on dry land for a few hours may take advantage of a watersports center with tennis courts, swimming pools, and a whirlpool.

Side Trips

THERE IS SO MUCH TO DO on Hilton Head Island that some tourists may have neither the time nor the inclination to venture off the island. But we urge you to do so if only for the afternoon. Adventurous visitors who explore surrounding towns and islands will be pleasantly surprised.

From eighteenth century homes with lush flower gardens to vast nature preserves, the Lowcountry has plenty to offer the day tripper.

Although all antebellum houses on Hilton Head have been destroyed, there are plenty of these gorgeous homes left in Beaufort, Bluffton, and Savannah. Unlike Hilton Head, each of these towns has a central area where visitors can park their cars and meander down quiet avenues of historical homes under a canopy of mossy live oaks. When azaleas and camellias bloom in early spring, there is no prettier sight on earth.

Beaufort

The venerable, exquisitely beautiful old town of Beaufort stands almost within eyesight of the northern shore of Hilton Head Island, across Port Royal Sound and up the Beaufort River. But to reach Beaufort by car, you must drive a distance of almost 30 miles from Hilton Head to the mainland, cross the long bridge over the Broad River, then to town. The drive takes you through lush Lowcountry landscapes and over wide waterways.

Once a summer resort for wealthy planters, now a popular location for the filming of *The Great Santini, The Big Chill, The Prince of Tides, Forrest Gump,* and many other Hollywood blockbusters, Beaufort has long attracted the rich and famous. The waterfront mansions along Beaufort Bay are some of the best preserved and most elaborate eighteenth and nineteenth century structures in the nation. Nature lovers should not miss the beach at Hunting Island State Park. Military buffs will want to visit the U.S. Marine Corps Recruit Depot at Parris Island. There is so much to see and do in Beaufort that you may want to spend the night at one of its excellent hotels or historical bed and breakfasts.

The second oldest town in South Carolina, Beaufort is the county seat of Beaufort County, in which Hilton Head Island, Daufuskie Island, Pinckney Island, and Bluffton are also located. Our guidebook *Beautiful Beaufort By The Sea,* available at Hilton Head bookstores, is indispensable for those who wish to visit Beaufort.

Bluffton

Bluffton is the very small town on the mainland, across the bridge from Hilton Head Island. As summer visitors to Hilton Head soon find, the island can become hot and humid during the months of July and August. Along with the heat come millions of pesky mosquitoes, which once carried life-threatening diseases such as malaria. Eighteenth and nineteenth century plantation families, who did not have the luxuries of air conditioning and bug spray, were understandably eager to leave the island during the summers. Bluffton was created as a summer refuge for these wealthy families, and named for the high bluffs upon which many of its houses were built.

The movement for secession from the Union had its roots in this small town. Summer resident Robert Barnwell Rhett began his long battle with the U.S. Government over the "Tariff of Abominations" which reduced cotton exports to England for the benefit of Northern manufacturers. He was a leading proponent of the "Bluffton Movement for a State Convention", and eventually helped to draft the Ordinance of Secession in his nearby home town of Beaufort.

When Rhett's efforts came to fruition, Bluffton residents were among the first to be affected. The 1861 landing of "the other" General Sherman and his thousands of Yankee troops on nearby Hilton Head Island forced most Blufftonians to head for the hills. Although they were not much of a threat to the hoards of Union soldiers stationed on Hilton Head, a small number of Confederates were stationed in Bluffton during the Civil War. Nighttime raids on Hilton Head were made by

Southern soldiers who had grown up on the island and were angry at the Union occupation of their family lands and homes. These raids so infuriated the Federal officers that they sent three vessels of troops to destroy Bluffton in 1863. When the planting families returned to Bluffton after the war, they found that all but 13 homes had been ruined.

Blufftonians went through many of the same hardships as Hilton Head families during the period of reconstruction. Bluffton even had its share of carpetbaggers in town. Local legend says that one especially unsavory character went by the name of "Reverend" Bannister. Harvard University gave him $6,000 to set up a school for freedmen, but the money somehow ended up in his pocket. When representatives from that venerable institution came to inspect the school, the "good" Reverend escaped through a chimney in his Bluffton home.

Another notable character in post Civil War Bluffton was Dr. Joseph H. Mellichamp. He had made a fairly good living as a doctor in the antebellum period, and decided to return to his practice after the war. Few people could afford to pay the doctor, but he would treat anyone of any race who showed up on his doorstep. Blufftonians like Doctor Mellichamp pulled together to rebuild their town. Today, the roads have improved and goods are no longer brought in by steamboat, but Bluffton has changed very little since the late nineteenth century.

With the development of nearby resorts, Bluffton has

grown in popularity as a destination for tourists who want to see a bit of the "Old South". Although close in proximity to bustling Hilton Head, Bluffton has lost none of its old-style charm. The Del Webb retirement community known as Sun City Hilton Head is currently being built near Bluffton. Blufftonians are holding their breaths to see if the town will continue to retain its character in the face of this influx.

Bluffton has the character a nineteenth-century Southern village. Take an afternoon off to stroll down the wide, almost deserted streets and admire the historical homes and lush gardens. Not only the homes, but the residents of this small town seem to come from an older, friendlier time. When you meet up with a Blufftonian, he or she will invariably offer a wide grin, say hello, and stand smiling until you return the greeting.

Visitors can glean some idea of Bluffton's pace by reading signs on local establishments. The library is open from 3:00 P.M. to 6:00 P.M. on Mondays, Wednesdays and Fridays—a schedule that's none too taxing for the local librarian and that works well with the Tuesday and Thursday opening of the banks. The proprietors of The Store, which opens sometime between 7:00 A.M. and noon, leave themselves plenty of time to sleep in if the spirit fails to move them. A bit of advice to motorists: do not exceed the speed limit in Bluffton. Members of the police force may all be complete gentlemen, but they are not so polite as to refrain from giving you a ticket.

Daufuskie Island

Daufuskie Island lies across Calibogue Sound, southwest of Hilton Head Island. Accessible only by boat, it remains a backwater of the Sea Islands but is emerging in fits and starts into the modern world. Europeans who sailed around the Sea Islands must have seen Daufuskie Island in the sixteenth and seventeenth centuries..

The British did not settle Daufuskie until the mideighteenth century due to threat of attack by the Spanish and Indians. Raiding parties of Yemassee Indians from Florida stopped at Daufuskie on the way to plantations near Charleston and back home. British scouts began to patrol the nearby waters, attacking any Yemassee plunderers who crossed their path. In 1715, a party of raiders was massacred by English settlers on the southern tip of Daufuskie. A few years later, this site was the scene of another battle between the British and Indians in which the Yemassee fared better. All of this fighting earned the southern tip of Daufuskie the name Bloody Point.

In 1740, King George II presented Captain John Mongin with the island of Daufuskie as a reward for his bravery in fighting Spanish pirates. His family started plantations on the island, where indigo was the primary crop. During the Revolutionary War, Daufuskie planters remained staunchly Tory, not wanting to lose the indigo subsidies given them by the British government. Neighbors on Hilton Head Island, who were primarily Patriots, nicknamed the island "Little Bermuda."

Skirmishes between residents of the two islands were inevitable. In 1781, a Captain Martinangel from Daufuskie shot Hilton Head planter Charles Davant to death. Davant's dying words to his son were, "get Martinangel". His family and friends were more than happy to oblige. They formed a war party of islanders, later called "The Bloody Legion" in Tory newspapers. Martinangel's home was raided and the Anglophile murdered.

Daufuskie's post-Revolutionary War history mirrored that of Hilton Head until the 1950s. Unlike Hilton Head, Daufuskie still remains a quiet place, populated primarily by descendants of the African slaves who once worked the cotton plantations there. The Gullah dialect spoken by Daufuskie residents can still be heard today. The traditional occupations of the islanders are fishing, farming, and oystering. Pat Conroy's best-selling novel, *The Water is Wide*, tells of his experiences as a secondary school teacher on Daufuskie in 1970 and of his sometimes frustrating interactions with young Daufuskie students and the Beaufort County educational authorities.

In the 1980s, the resorts of Melrose and Haig Point brought the outside world to Daufuskie. Still a far cry from fast-paced Hilton Head, these areas are juxtaposed against the rural backdrop of the traditional culture. A trip around the non-resort areas of Daufuskie will show the visitor that the traditional residents still enjoy the tranquil lifestyle of this isolated, rural Sea Island where nothing much has happened for hundreds of years.

Pinckney Island

If you want to see what the Sea Islands looked like before humans set foot here, take a short trip to Pinckney Island National Wildlife Preserve, accessible by car at the bridge approach to Hilton Head Island. This 4,000-acre preserve of unspoiled land has a short car path and about 14 miles of hiking and biking trails. There is no better spot for wildlife viewing within an hour of Hilton Head.

The family that owned the island from the late 1700s had, as you might have guessed, the surname Pinckney. The Pinckneys were an extraordinary family of statesmen, botanists, and intellectuals, and their descendants can still be found all over the Lowcountry. The most famous was Charles Cotesworth Pinckney, an accomplished lawyer and Revolutionary War general. Pinckney was one of the leading proponents of the U.S. Constitution and attended the Constitutional Convention in Philadelphia. George Washington offered Pinckney the position of Secretary of State, which Pinckney refused because he felt he should stay close to home to care for his daughters. In the early nineteenth century, the Federalist Party twice chose Pinckney as their presidential candidate, but he was twice defeated, once by Thomas Jefferson and again by James Madison.

After the death of Charles Cotesworth Pinckney, his niece Harriott administered the island plantation until the Civil War forced her off the island at the age of 87. After the war, her relatives successfully petitioned the government for a return of all lands. They argued that Miss Pinckney could not have fought in any battles, due to her sex and advanced age, and that her uncle Charles Cotesworth Pinckney had been a fine patriot. Ulysses S. Grant himself recommended that the island be returned to the Pinckneys, which it was.

After the Civil War, the Pinckneys tried to run the plantation as their ancestors had done before them, but were unable to keep it functioning. Black moonshiners, who lived on the island in the 1920s and '30s, were a bit more successful in their endeavors. In the late 1930s, a successful Northern banker bought the island as a private hunting reserve. He brought pheasants to the island, but they have since been killed or sent back to the midwest. James Madison Barker, rather ironically named after one of the presidential candidates who defeated Charles Cotesworth Pinckney, was the next owner. He turned Pinckney Island over to the Federal government. It became a National Wildlife Refuge in 1975.

Savannah

The bustling seaport city of Savannah, Georgia, is 30 miles from Hilton Head Island. From its modest beginnings as a colony of 144 Englishmen, to its later position as one of the commercial centers of the antebellum South, to its present-day status as a busy port and tourist destination, Savannah has been an important city throughout the history of America. Visitors can admire greenery and flowers in Savannah's 24 town squares, which were all part of General James E. Oglethorpe's original plan for the city. Savannah also has the largest historic district of any city in the United States. Over 1,500 historically significant structures have survived two devastating fires, neither of which was set by General W.T. Sherman. In fact, Savannah so impressed Sherman that he "gave" the city to President Lincoln as a Christmas present in 1864. It is beyond the scope of this book to present an account of Savannah's rich history and points of interest, but suffice it to say that a trip to this extraordinary city would be a high point of any visit to the Lowcountry.

Other Good Things to Know

FOLKS WHO VISITED Hilton Head Island or retired there in the "good old days" of the early 1960s are wont to point out how nicely removed from the hustle and bustle of urban America it was then. Now they complain about the traffic on the island, which at times does become bumper to bumper on Highway 278. A lot of things were different when Sea Pines was the only gated community on the island. Oceanfront lots could originally be bought for $6,500; hotel accommodations were a choice between the William Hilton Inn and the Seacrest Motel.

You won't find any more of those bargains today. But you will find what you could not find then, as full an array of pleasant choices as possible in an oceanfront resort community in the United States. Here are a few things you might find useful to know when you visit:

Medical Care

Hilton Head Hospital, Hospital Center Boulevard off Highway 278, 681-6122. There is no need to panic if you have a medical emergency on Hilton Head Island. This thriving, modern hospital facility, located at the north end of the island, has 65 participating physicians. Urgent care centers are located at the hospital (689-8281) and at the south end of the island at 10 Pope Avenue, Sea Pines Circle (785-9400).

Pharmacies

Burke's Main Street Pharmacy, 1101 Main Street, 681-2622, offers home therapy and medical equipment rental as well as prescription service.

Nash Drugs, a discount pharmacy with three locations at The Market Place (785-5241), The Plaza at Shelter Cove (785-3171), and Coligny Plaza (785-7737), provides free delivery of orders over $10, senior citizen discounts, film developing, and beach supplies.

Sea Pines Pharmacy, 79 Lighthouse Road, 671-6138. This computerized pharmacy has 24-hour emergency service, photo processing, photocopier, and sundries.

Suggestions for Further Reading

Beautiful Beaufort By The Sea, by Marie Bernice La Touche and George Graham Trask, is the definitive guidebook to nearby Beaufort, the famous and historic coastal town you won't want to miss when you explore the area.

Biography of an Island, by Merrill G. Christophersen, gives a complete history of Pinckney Island and the people who owned it.

Coastal Ghosts, by Nancy Rhyne, tells eerie tales of supernatural visitations on Hilton Head and other Low-country locales. Read all about the Baynards and the Daufuskie bigfoot.

Department of the South, Hilton Head Island in the

Civil War, by Robert Carse, is a fascinating account of the Union occupation of Hilton Head during the Civil War. This book gives details of the day-to-day lives of soldiers living on the island and tells entertaining stories of the often incompetent commanders leading them. A must for Civil War history buffs.

Hilton Head, A Sea Island Chronicle, by Virginia C. Holmgren, covers the history of Hilton Head from pre-historic days until just before the first resort was built. Sections on the antebellum and reconstruction period are quite extensive.

Nature Guide to the Carolina Coast, by Peter Meyer, a practical, easy-to-read guide for beachcombers and weekend naturalists.

Profits and Politics in Paradise: The Development of Hilton Head, by Michael Danielson, tells the intriguing story of the combination of money and ego that stands behind the creation of modern-day Hilton Head.

Rehearsal for Reconstruction, by Willie Lee Rose, is a superb history of the Sea Islands during the Civil War and reconstruction focusing on the lives of freed Low-country slaves. This book has won three prestigious awards for historical literature.

Sands of Time, by Margaret Greer, gives an overview of the history of Beaufort County in an attractive pictorial book.

Sea Island Roots: African Presence in the Carolinas and

Georgia, Twining & Baird, is a collection of essays on the Gullah culture and the history of black people in the Sea Islands.

South Carolina and the Sea, by J. Percival Petit, gives an account of South Carolina's nautical history, from the arrival of the first Spanish explorers until modern times.

Tideland Treasures, by Todd Ballantine, a naturalist's guide to beaches and salt marshes of the Lowcountry, beautifully illustrated and hand-lettered by the author.

The Water is Wide, by Pat Conroy, is the semi-autobiographical story of a schoolteacher from the mainland who is sent to Daufuskie Island. The trials of being a new teacher are compounded by the differences in culture between Conroy and his black students. Most of Conroy's other books, including *The Great Santini, The Prince of Tides,* and *Beach Music,* are set in the South Carolina Lowcountry centered around nearby Beaufort, Conroy's childhood home.

Index

About Author and Artist

Rebecca Kaufmann Crowley has the extraordinary ability to use superbly both sides of her brain. She came to writing this guidebook after first proving herself as a member of the Peace Corps teaching secondary-school mathematics in Botswana and as a Certified Public Accountant in South Carolina. A native of Durham, New Hampshire, and a graduate of Swarthmore College in Pennsylvania, Rebecca reclaimed her Southern heritage by building a house with her husband, Steve, on Fripp Island, South Carolina. While there she fell in love with the surrounding South Carolina Sea Islands and wrote this book. She and Steve have now returned to Botswana, where Rebecca practices accounting in Gaborone and dreams of writing another book.

Jackson Causey styles himself a realist painter of the American scene, painting God's creation and its beauty. A chronicler of human achievements and our heritage, Jackson is a South Carolina native whose works are displayed nationwide. Jackson and his wife, Edie, maintain his studio/gallery in their home in Beaufort, South Carolina.

Colophon

Coastal Villages Press is dedicated to helping
to preserve the timeless values of traditional
places along our nation's Atlantic coast—
building houses to endure through
the centuries; living in harmony
with the natural environment;
honoring history, culture,
family and friends—
and helping to
make
these
values
relevant
today.
This
book
was
completed on
August 10, 1995, at
Beaufort, South Carolina. It was
set in Caslon, used in the first printing
of the Declaration of Independence in 1776.

What Others Say
About Our Guidebooks

"Comprehensive, consumer-friendly. Provides help without overpowering. Offers details that we might never have heard or might have forgotten." Hilton Head *Island Packet.*

"Handsome and comprehensive. Absorbing information. No-nonsense approach. Elegant layout." *Carolina Style* magazine.

"Great resource to have on hand. This guidebook has historical and visual appeal." *The Nantucket Beacon.*

"Packed with good and useful information." *Nantucket Map & Legend.*

"Fact-packed, full of colorful descriptions." Nantucket *Inquirer and Mirror.*